DEVELOPING LEARNING AGILITY

DEVELOPING LEARNING AGILITY

Using the Burke Assessments

DAVID F. HOFF AND **W. WARNER BURKE**

© 2022 by Hogan Press, a division of Hogan Assessment Systems, Inc.

All rights reserved. No part of this publication may be reproduced, distributed, or transmitted in any form or by any means, including photocopying, recording, or other electronic or mechanical methods, without prior written permission of the author, except by a reviewer who wishes to quote brief passages in connection with a review written for inclusion in a magazine, newspaper or broadcast.

Printed in the United States of America.

For information, contact Hogan Press
11 S. Greenwood, Tulsa OK 74120
hoganassessments.com

ISBN: 979-8-9856452-0-0

Cover design by 99designs
Typeset by Progressive Publishing Services

This book is dedicated to my grandchildren, Ryder, Wren and Birdie Clarissa Mari Jane Hoff. I watch them try new things and fail, fail and finally succeed or move on to something else. I watch them use feedback whether solicited or not and see its impact on their performance. I see the gears turning as they apply different frameworks until they find the one that's appropriate to this situation. May they have an unquenchable thirst for learning and a self confidence that allows them to see and achieve the impossible.

*Special thanks to
Kristen Eckhart and Kim McGuiness
for their contributions to this book.*

CONTENTS

PROLOGUE	1
CHAPTER 1 An Overview of Learning Agility	3
CHAPTER 2 Selecting the Right Version of the Burke Learning Agility Assessment	9
CHAPTER 3 Validating the Burke Assessment Report Through Directive and Nondirective Coaching	25
CHAPTER 4 Rick Croson: A Life Example of Learning Agility in Action	33
CHAPTER 5 Theory and Research on Learning Agility	45
CHAPTER 6 *Flexibility*	73
CHAPTER 7 *Speed*	87
CHAPTER 8 *Experimenting*	101
CHAPTER 9 *Performance* and *Interpersonal Risk Taking*	109
CHAPTER 10 *Collaborating*	129
CHAPTER 11 *Information Gathering*	139

CHAPTER 12
Feedback Seeking — 145

CHAPTER 13
Reflecting — 157

EPILOGUE — 165

REFERENCES — 169

ABOUT THE AUTHORS — 175

INDEX — 177

PROLOGUE

Developing Learning Agility: Using the Burke Assessments is intended to give the reader a set of practical activities they can apply in work situations to develop the 38 items found in the assessments. This book complements *Learning Agility: The Key to Leader Potential*, our first book on this subject. In that book we defined learning agility, summarized the research behind the assessments, and described what the demonstration of each of the dimensions looks like in a work setting and how learning agility could be applied to different human resource systems in an organization.

After learning about the nine dimensions of the Burke Assessment and that each of the 38 items on the assessment are behavioral, the next step is learning how to develop each of those items or behaviors. That is the focus of this book. Assessments is plural, as there are now three versions of the assessment. The first chapter is a review of the basics of learning agility. Chapter 2 explains the advantages and disadvantages of the three different assessments. How the assessment will be applied will determine which version will be the most appropriate to use. Chapter 3 describes how a coach or a facilitator might discuss an assessment taker's report with them: how the coach would try to "validate" the information in the report, determine the most important areas for development, and determine how to structure that development.

Assessment takers who are wrestling with information in their assessment report are often looking for an example of what learning agility looks like as it is happening in the world. Chapter 4 is that example. Captain Rick Croson is a charter boat captain who leads daily trips for small groups of fishers off the coast of North Carolina. Rick demonstrates an amazing ability to navigate the daily ambiguities of a career on the water. He constantly reinvents his product, its delivery, and his consumer. This example is from a very different context than how learning agility is applied in the public and private sector, and that is by design.

For our more academic readers, we wanted to include an in-depth review of the evolution of the field of organization development and, more specifically, learning agility. Warner Burke has done a masterful job of summarizing that literature and subtly connecting elements of that work to the emerging area of learning agility. The next eight chapters examine each of the nine dimensions of the Burke Assessment at length. We chose to combine *Performance* and *Interpersonal* into one chapter on *Risk Taking*, so there are eight dimension chapters. Each chapter focuses on four or five behavioral descriptions and gives the reader specific activities they can use to develop those behaviors.

We hope you enjoy our second effort to expand the study of learning agility. This time we expanded the number of tools available and demonstrated how these 38 behaviors can be developed. We welcome your feedback.

CHAPTER 1

AN OVERVIEW OF LEARNING AGILITY

While the focus of this book is on developing learning agility, we need to start with a review of some of the ideas introduced in *Learning Agility: The Key to Leader Potential*, which was published in 2017. Our focus on learning agility is based on decades of research by Warner Burke, PhD, who is a professor at Columbia University and a recognized expert in industrial-organizational (I-O) psychology. Burke developed an assessment of learning agility that consists of 38 items measuring nine dimensions. When *Learning Agility: The Key to Leader Potential* was published, there were a few measures of learning agility in the marketplace. Since then, the term "learning agility" has been co-opted for use as a verb, an adjective, and an adverb as well as used in phrases such as "agile organizations," any and all of which may create confusion for consumers in organizations.

In Chapter 1 of *Learning Agility: The Key to Leader Potential*, we explained that the premise behind Burke's approach to learning agility was that it did not require organization-wide adoption. Burke's measure of learning agility could be implemented at the individual, team, business unit, or organizational level. Our definition of learning agility is "Finding yourself in a situation where you have never been before, you don't know what to do, and yet you figure it out." Individuals can and do demonstrate learning agility on their own in organizations. In the first edition, we introduced DeRue et al. (2012a; 2012b) and shared their model explaining learning agility. One important aspect of their model is context. Context matters. When applying this idea to implementing learning agility in an organization, it is easier when the organization's vernacular, behavior, and systems support learning agility behaviors.

In *Learning Agility*, we tried to clarify that there is a distinction between learning ability and learning agility. Learning ability is cognitive agility. Learning agility is being able to flexibly handle both known and unknown situations. Learning ability is important to a point, but once that threshold is reached, a greater amount of *learning ability* is not necessarily going to translate into greater *learning agility*.

We then defined the nine dimensions of learning agility as the following:

- *Flexibility* – Being open to new ideas and proposing new solutions.
- *Speed* – Acting on ideas quickly so that those that are not working are discarded and other possibilities are accelerated.
- *Experimenting* – Trying out new behaviors (approaches, ideas) to determine what is effective.
- *Performance Risk Taking* – Seeking new activities (tasks, assignments, roles) that provide opportunities to be challenged.
- *Interpersonal Risk Taking* – Discussing differences with others in ways that lead to learning and change.
- *Collaborating* – Finding ways to work with others that generate unique challenges for learning.
- *Information Gathering* – Using various methods to remain current in one's area of expertise.
- *Feedback Seeking* – Asking others for feedback on one's ideas and overall performance.
- *Reflecting* – Slowing down to evaluate one's own performance to be more effective.

Of course, there are a few other foundational ideas that contribute to our understanding of learning agility. DeRue et al. stated that we all have identifiable and individual differences, which they called antecedents. These antecedents are part of who we are and precede any learning agility opportunity. According to DeRue, learning agility consists of *Speed* and *Flexibility*. Burke's research confirmed the importance of *Speed* and

Flexibility, but expanded on DeRue's model to define seven other capabilities. Per Burke, *Speed* and *Flexibility* are the drivers of learning agility and support the other seven dimensions.

Burke's research identified two other considerations that are important to learning agility: skill and motivation. Skill is the starting point in a learning agility situation. Being more skillful does not necessarily translate to being more learning agile; skill is where we start. Motivation is about how important learning agility is to us. Someone with a higher level of motivation as it relates to learning agility is going to expend a greater amount of discretionary effort than someone who is less motivated. There is no evaluation attached to skill or motivation, just a description.

That summarizes the research base for learning agility; next, let us look at how it is measured.

THE BURKE ASSESSMENTS
SELF-REPORTS

The Burke Self-Report assessments consist of two versions (the Burke Learning Agility Inventory and Burke Learning Agility Inventory Expanded Version), based on the same 38 items found in all the Burke Learning Agility assessments. The results of The Burke Learning Agility Inventory Expanded Version assessment were normed. The original norm group consisted of 394 middle- and senior-level managers from a range of organizations and industries. The sample was primarily U.S.-based. The sample had almost an equal number of males and females. The original norm group was refreshed in October 2019. This new sample consists of 445 individuals holding positions from individual contributor to senior manager, representing a variety of functions and industries. The sample is approximately half female and half male. Approximately half of the sample participants are from the United States and half are from outside of the United States.

MULTI-RATER VERSIONS

Since *Learning Agility: The Key to Leader Potential* was written, two additional assessments have been developed: the Burke Learning Agility Survey (LAS) 180® and the Burke Learning Agility Survey (LAS) 360®.

The Burke 180 measures the self and one other perspective. This is typically the supervisor, but any other person can complete the assessment. The Burke 360 assessment can accommodate up to five perspectives. The report formats of the self-assessment and the multi-rater assessments are different. Chapter 2 of this book compares the different versions of the assessment and covers how to select the right version. The two multi-rater versions of the assessment use raw scores instead of normed scores.

BURKE'S RESEARCH

Chapters 2 and 3 of *Learning Agility: The Key to Leader Potential* focused on the original research leading to the Burke Learning Agility Inventory (LAI), the first assessment developed from Burke's research. That book included a description of a criterion validity study of hedge fund managers. The study determined that people who scored higher on the Burke LAI were rated as better performers. After learning of this finding, a global consumer products company asked if the Burke LAI could be used to determine learning agility for individual contributors, a category that was not included in the original norm group. The global consumer products company provided a sample of 200 individual contributors, and the results of that study and those findings are described in Chapter 5 of this book. At the time, we believed there would be a relationship between learning agility and personality. Together, E.A.S.I-Consult® and Hogan (the providers of the Hogan Personality Assessment) performed a study to examine the relationship between personality and learning agility. The results of that study are described in Chapter 5.

OVERVIEW

The second section of *Learning Agility: The Key to Leader Potential* was devoted to examples of what each of the dimensions of learning agility look like inside organizations and at their different levels. Each fictional situation described an individual who was not demonstrating learning agility at work. Learning agility was then introduced into each situation, but not expanded in a way that would show how capabilities could be developed. The third section of *Learning Agility: The Key to Leader Potential* described six different applications of the Burke Self-Report to human resource activities such as coaching, leadership development, and succession planning.

In this book, separate chapters are devoted to developing learning agility by dimension. We will take the focus down to the item level and give specific examples of how someone can develop each of those items and do so in a way that is specific and measurable. *Developing Learning Agility: Using the Burke Assessment* builds on the ideas introduced in *Learning Agility: The Key to Leader Potential*. This book is intended for both leaders and coaches for the purposes of development, including their own. Chapter 2, on selecting the correct version of the assessment, and Chapter 3, on validating the assessment results, may be more pertinent to coaches or human resources professionals. Chapter 5, on research, may be of more interest if you have a research background. Research is something that differentiates our assessments from others, so in the spirit of transparency we chose to include it.

The growth in the number of versions of the Burke assessments is exciting. The assessments are being used globally and are beginning to be translated into other languages, and Burke tools are already being applied at the team and organizational levels, which means there will continue to be opportunities to expand the research base of the Burke tools.

CHAPTER 2

SELECTING THE RIGHT VERSION OF THE BURKE LEARNING AGILITY ASSESSMENT

When E.A.S.I-Consult® introduced the Burke Learning Agility Inventory® Standard version, it was easy to answer the question, "Which is the right version of the assessment for my organization to use?" There was only one assessment at that time.

The plan was to add a multi-rater version of the assessment. In response to customer requests, based on their desired applications, we created four versions of what we are calling the Burke Suite of Learning Agility products that are now available:

 Burke Learning Agility Inventory (LAI) Standard

 Burke Learning Agility Inventory (LAI) Expanded

 Burke Learning Agility Inventory Survey (LAS) 180

 Burke Learning Agility Inventory Survey (LAS) 360

9

All four versions of the assessment use the same 38 questions. There are five questions each for *Speed* and *Flexibility*, and the other seven dimensions have four questions each. What follows are definitions of the nine dimensions. You will find a list like this in the report for each version of the assessment.

DIMENSIONS

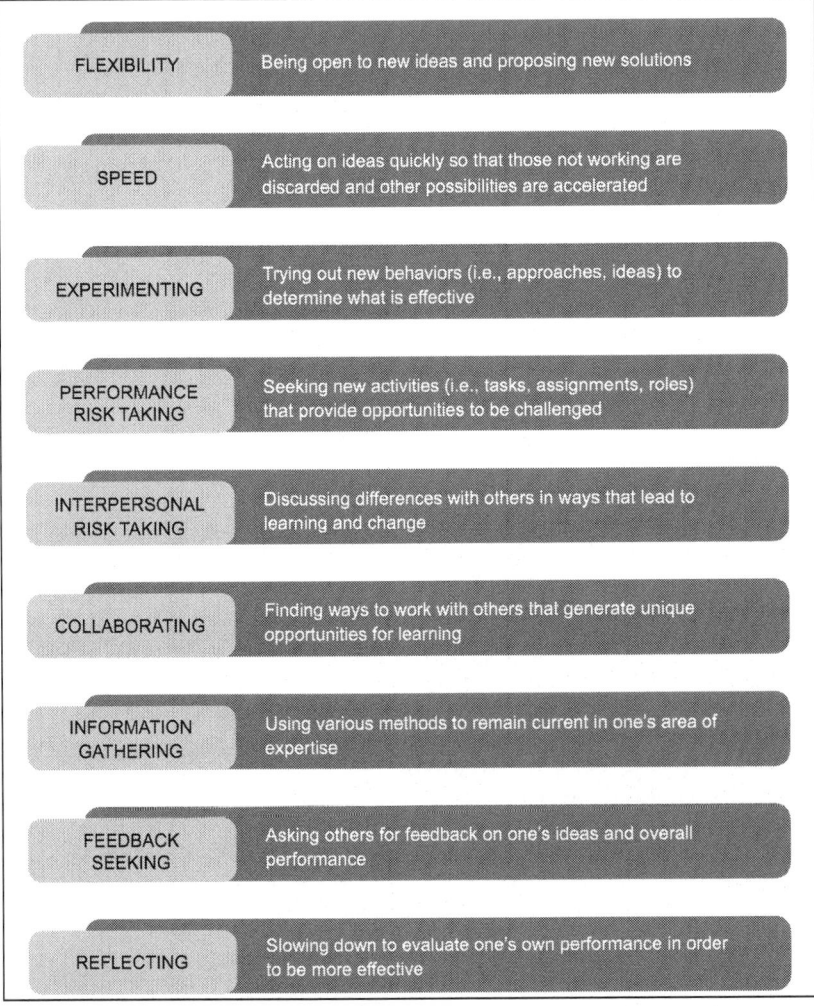

FLEXIBILITY	Being open to new ideas and proposing new solutions
SPEED	Acting on ideas quickly so that those not working are discarded and other possibilities are accelerated
EXPERIMENTING	Trying out new behaviors (i.e., approaches, ideas) to determine what is effective
PERFORMANCE RISK TAKING	Seeking new activities (i.e., tasks, assignments, roles) that provide opportunities to be challenged
INTERPERSONAL RISK TAKING	Discussing differences with others in ways that lead to learning and change
COLLABORATING	Finding ways to work with others that generate unique opportunities for learning
INFORMATION GATHERING	Using various methods to remain current in one's area of expertise
FEEDBACK SEEKING	Asking others for feedback on one's ideas and overall performance
REFLECTING	Slowing down to evaluate one's own performance in order to be more effective

Burke Learning Agility Dimensions and Definitions

All versions of the assessment use the same Likert scale, which asks the respondent how often they demonstrate that item, with options ranging from 1 (not at all) to 7 (always). The only difference between the Burke Self-Report and the multi-rater versions (LAS 180 and LAS 360) is that the "other raters" are asked the question, "How often does **this person** demonstrate this behavior?" There is also an option to indicate "not applicable."

EXAMPLE OF BURKE SELF-REPORT QUESTION

How often do you demonstrate the following behavior?

○ 1 - Never

○ 2 - Once in a while

○ 3 - Sometimes

○ 4 - Fairly Often

○ 5 - Often

○ 6 - Constantly

○ 7 - Always

Sample Likert Scale-Frequency

How are the two versions of the Burke Learning Agility Inventory (LAI) different? Both versions of the self-report assessment are normed. A normative, or norm, group is the sample of assessment takers who are representative of the population for whom the assessment is intended; this allows the results to be reported as percentiles. The initial norm group for the earliest Burke assessment consisted of primarily middle- and senior-level managers from a variety of organizations, mostly from the United States. In October 2019, a new norm group was created, consisting of participants who held individual contributors through senior-level manager positions. The sample was equally divided between participants who resided in the United States and participants who resided outside of the United States. The norming for both studies used the Burke Learning Agility Expanded Version of the assessment.

BURKE LAI PROFILE BY DIMENSION

The two versions of the Burke LAI self-assessment reports start with an overall score. In the example below, the assessment taker scored at the 73rd percentile. This means they scored higher than 73% of the overall population and that 27% of the population scored higher than them. The score puts this person in the "high" range on the assessment.

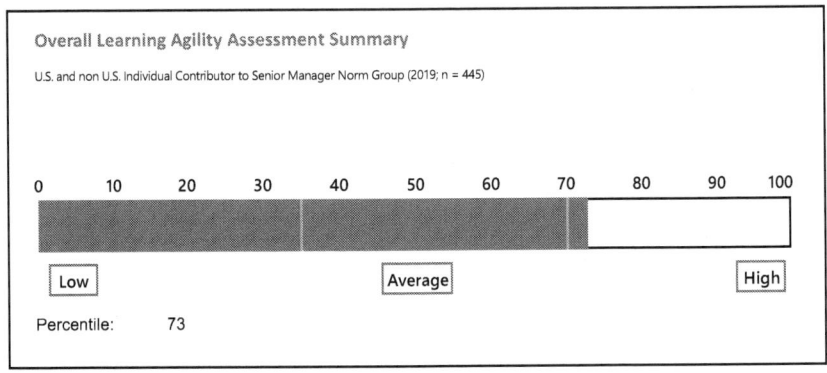

Sample Overall Score

The second profile by dimension that is received by people who take either version of the Burke LAI is a profile by dimension, an example of which is seen below. This profile shows the assessment taker that they have several strong capabilities: *Performance* and *Interpersonal Risk Taking*, *Collaborating*, and *Feedback Seeking*. There are other dimensions that the assessment taker might want to strengthen (*Information Gathering* and *Reflecting*).

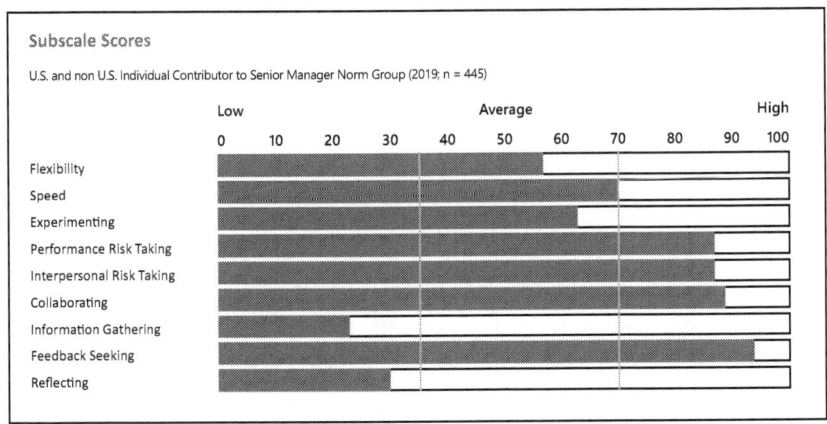

Profile by Dimension

SELECTING THE RIGHT VERSION OF THE BURKE LEARNING AGILITY ASSESSMENT

The Burke Self-Report Standard (LAI Standard) and the Burke Self-Report Expanded (LAI Expanded Version) differ in the output of the assessment, which is the report. The report generated by the Burke Self-Report Standard provides descriptions of results at the dimension level only. Organizations that want to use this assessment as part of a selection process typically find that this information meets their needs.

In the following example, the assessment taker scored in the 57th percentile, putting them in the average category.

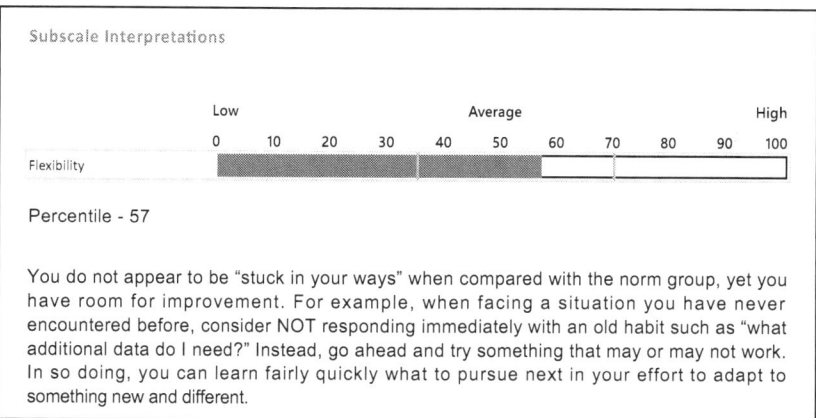

Example of Burke Self-Report Standard Version Dimension Report

BURKE SELF-REPORT EXPANDED VERSION DIMENSION AND ITEM REPORT

The report generated from the Burke Self-Report Expanded version provides information at the dimension and item levels. Organizations use this version for leadership development, coaching, performance management, onboarding, and succession planning. What follows is an example from the Burke (LAI) Expanded version for the dimension of *Flexibility*. The Expanded version's report consists of nine pages, with one page for each of the nine dimensions. Each page contains a summary paragraph at the top of the page that describes the person's overall capability on that dimension. The bullet points that follow, five in the case of *Flexibility*, refer to how the person rated themselves on that particular item on the assessment and provide suggestions for how the person can improve on each of the items.

DEVELOPING LEARNING AGILITY

Subscale Interpretations

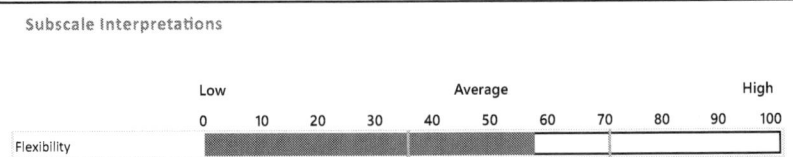

Percentile - 57

You do not appear to be "stuck in your ways" when compared with the norm group, yet you have room for improvement. For example, when facing a situation you have never encountered before, consider NOT responding immediately with an old habit such as "what additional data do I need?" Instead, go ahead and try something that may or may not work. In so doing, you can learn fairly quickly what to pursue next in your effort to adapt to something new and different.

- You look at a broad range of options before deciding the one to pursue. Others see you as a person who will help expand their thinking. Some people may describe you as an "out of the box" thinker.

- One of your capabilities is handling multiple-priorities simultaneously. Moving among multiple projects or tasks in a single day or week is energizing and provides you with variety. Others will seek you out because of your ability to comfortably shift among several priorities.

- On occasion, you offer solutions that others see as innovative. This is something you should try to do more often. Take a chance that others will like your ideas. Your input can help others in their efforts to solve problems. If you do this, people will seek you out as a resource on their teams and projects.

- Sometimes, you see similarities where others only see differences. Others appreciate the value that adds to a group that is trying to reach consensus. People working on change or transformation projects will seek your participation if they are confident of your willingness to describe the similarities you see.

- Describing the differences that exist among points of view is an ability you sometimes display. Others listen more closely when you state those differences not always apparent to them. People will seek your expertise to describe the differences stated during a discussion if they are confident you will play this role.

Improving in this area will allow you to apply different frameworks to better understand the situations and solve problems.

Example of Burke Self-Report Expanded Version Dimension and Item Report

BURKE LEARNING AGILITY SURVEY (LAS) 180 AND 360

There are also two versions of the Burke multi-rater assessments, or Burke Learning Agility Surveys (LAS). Both surveys use the same 38 questions, and the structure of the reports for both versions is the same. For users who are familiar with other 360 products, the report is similar.

The components of the report are the following:
- An initial diagram summarizing the dimension level scoring by the participant and their other raters (see Spider Diagram from Burke Report). The self-assessment is in light gray; the combination of all the other raters (all, except self) appears in a darker gray. In the Burke LAS 180, there are only two perspectives (self and other). In the Burke LAS 360, there can be as many as five perspectives.
- A difference between a self-rated score and the other raters' combined score of 1.0 or greater can be considered significant, and the assessment taker may want to examine that difference. In this example, the difference in scoring on the dimensions *Speed, Performance Risk Taking, Interpersonal Risk Taking, Collaborating,* and *Information Gathering* is 1.0 or greater, so those dimensions should be given additional attention.

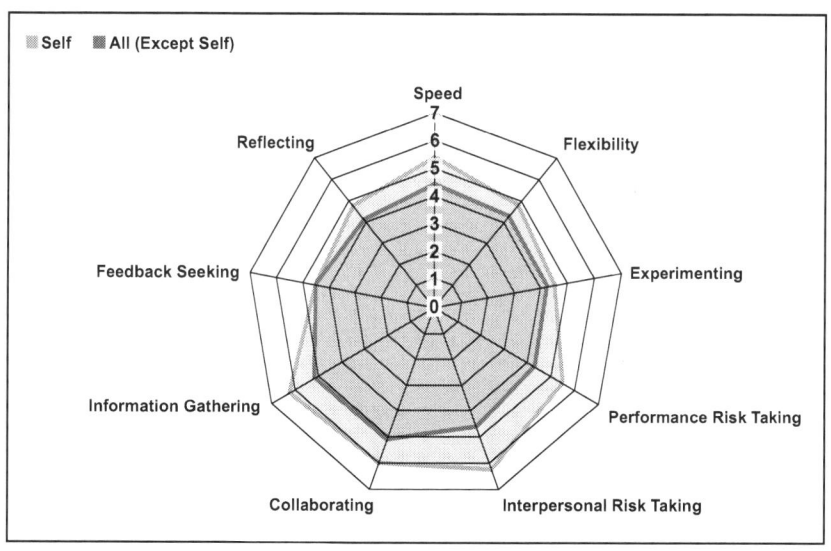

Spider Diagram from Burke Report

- The next several pages in either the Burke LAS 180 or Burke LAS 360 report provide a summary of each dimension from each perspective. In the Burke LAS 180, there are only two perspectives (self and other), while in the Burke LAS 360 there could be up to five perspectives.

SUMMARY BY LEARNING AGILITY DIMENSION
BURKE LAS 180

The first example is from the Burke LAS 180 and shows the *Flexibility* and *Speed* dimensions. There is not a significant difference between the self and other ratings (a difference greater than 1.0 is considered significant). The bulleted statements below the bar graph describe how a person might behave if they scored high or low on that dimension.

The Burke LAS 180 is in some ways a combination of the self-report and multi-rater report as it adds only one other rater besides the assessment taker. That other person is generally the assessment taker's manager, which is a very important perspective to receive.

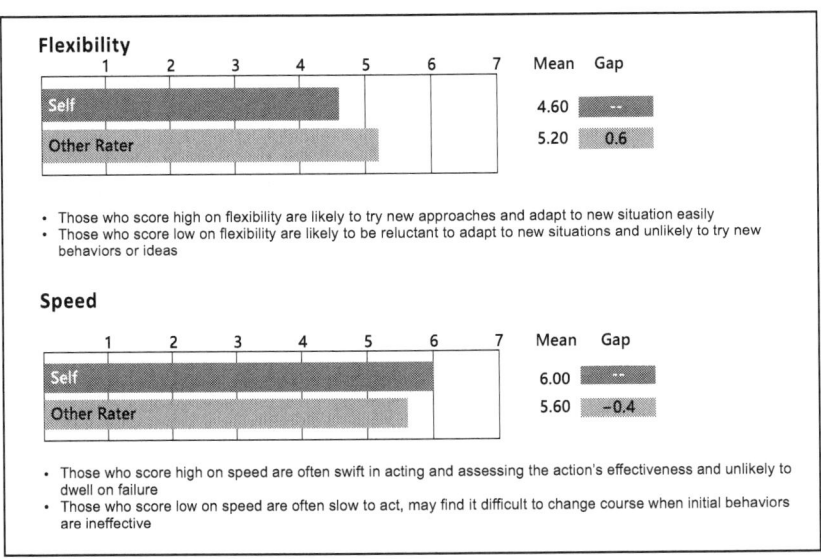

Two Dimensions from the Burke 180 Report at the Dimension Level

BURKE LAS 360

The next example is from the Burke LAS 360 and shows the *Flexibility* and *Speed* dimensions. In both dimensions there is a significant difference (greater than 1.0) between the self and the manager ratings. This indicates an area requiring further consideration. The bulleted statements below the bar graph describe how a person might behave if they scored high or low on that dimension.

SELECTING THE RIGHT VERSION OF THE BURKE LEARNING AGILITY ASSESSMENT

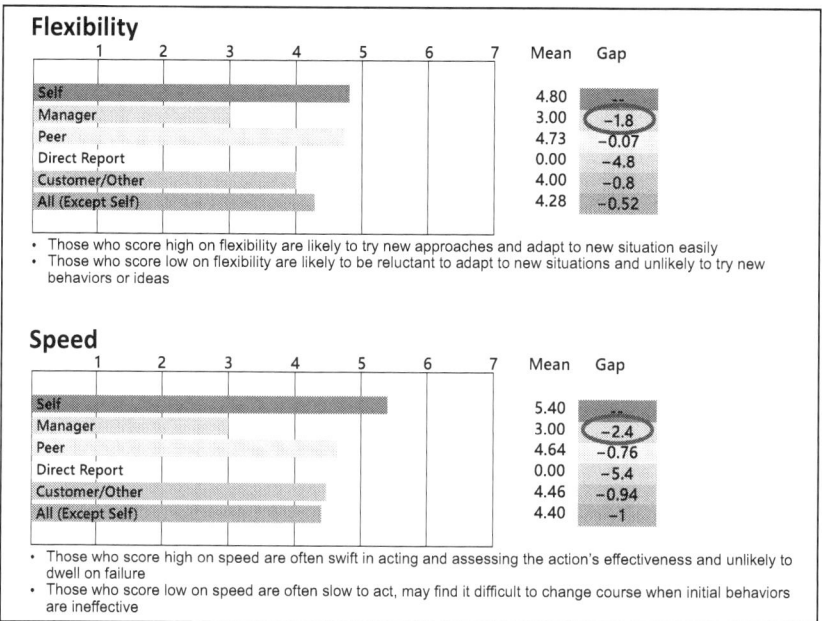

Two Dimensions from the Burke 360 Report at the Dimension Level

AGGREGATED SCORES

In the next section of both the Burke LAS 180 and Burke LAS 360, items from the assessment are aggregated in four ways: highest scores, lowest scores, unrecognized strengths, and blind spots.

HIGHEST AND LOWEST SCORES

The first chart titled "Highest Scores as Seen by the Other Rater" aggregates the five items that others rated the assessment taker highest on. For the Burke 180, the score is that given by the other rater only. The Burke 360 gives the *average* scores of the five highest rated items as rated by others.

The second chart ("Lowest Scores as Seen by the Other Rater") does the opposite and aggregates the assessment taker's five lowest-rated items as rated by others. Again, the Burke LAS 180 gives the score of the only other rater, and the Burke 360 gives the *average* scores of the five items lowest rated by others.

Highest Scores as Seen by the Other Rater			
Rank	Scoring Category	Item	Score
1	Information Gathering	Collect data to increase my knowledge, evaluate my progress, and inform my next steps.	7.00
2	Collaborating	Work with colleagues from different backgrounds or job functions to share perspectives.	7.00
3	Speed	React well to unexpected problems.	6.00
4	Performance Risk Taking	Volunteer for assignments or projects that involve the possibility of failure.	6.00
5	Collaborating	Collaborate with people in other parts of the organization.	6.00
Lowest Scores as Seen by the Other Rater			
Rank	Scoring Category	Item	Score
1	Feedback Seeking	Ask my peers to provide me with feedback on my performance.	3.00
2	Experimenting	Experiment with unproven ideas by testing them out.	3.00
3	Interpersonal Risk Taking	Bring up problems and tough issues with others.	4.00
4	Experimenting	Try different approaches to see which one generates the best results.	4.00
5	Information Gathering	Read trade journals, newspaper articles, books, or other sources to stay informed.	4.00

Highest and Lowest Scores

UNRECOGNIZED STRENGTHS AND BLIND SPOTS

The next chart lists the five items for which others gave the assessment taker a higher rating than the assessment taker gave themselves, or "unrecognized strengths." For the Burke LAS 180, these are the five items with the greatest difference in scoring, or "gap," between scores given by the other rater and the assessment taker. For the Burke LAS 360, the "all" rating is the average of the five scores given by others.

The second chart presents "blind spots," or the five items for which the assessment taker's self-ratings were higher than others' ratings of them. For the Burke LAS 180, these are the five items with the greatest difference in scoring between the self-rating and the score of the other rater. Since, in this case, the self-rating is always higher, the gaps between the scores will all be negative. The Burke LAS 360 gives the average of the others' ratings. Again, the gap will always be negative.

		Unrecognized Strengths			
Rank	Scoring Category	Item	All (Except Self)	Self	Gap
1	Feedback Seeking	Discuss my potential for advancement within the organization with my manager.	5.20	2.00	3.20
2	Experimenting	Experiment with unproven ideas by testing them out.	4.00	3.00	1.00
3	Experimenting	Jump into action and learn by trial and error.	4.00	3.00	1.00
4	Feedback Seeking	Seek feedback from my manager about my performance.	4.83	4.00	0.83
5	Flexibility	Articulate seemingly competing ideas or perspectives.	4.71	4.00	0.71

		Blind Spots			
Rank	Scoring Category	Item	All (Except Self)	Self	Gap
1	Feedback Seeking	Ask my peers to provide me with feedback on my performance.	4.33	7.00	-2.67
2	Interpersonal Risk Taking	Discuss my mistakes with others.	3.38	6.00	-2.63
3	Speed	React well to unexpected problems.	3.75	6.00	-2.25
4	Performance Risk Taking	Take on new roles or assignments that are challenging.	4.88	7.00	-2.13
5	Interpersonal Risk Taking	Challenge others' ideas and opinions even when they are shared by many people.	4.89	7.00	-2.11

High and Low Scores and Unrecognized Strengths and Blind Spots

SUMMARY BY LEARNING AGILITY DIMENSION AND BY ITEM
BURKE LAS 180

The next section of the report lists the assessment taker's ratings by dimension and then by item. The dimensions of *Speed* and *Flexibility* each have five associated item scores; all the other dimensions have four items, as in our example of the *Feedback Seeking* dimension. It is in this section of the report where the discrepancies between the assessment taker's self-rating and others' ratings may be more pronounced. The specificity of the items allows the person being assessed to know what aspect of *Feedback Seeking*, for example, they need to focus on improving.

DEVELOPING LEARNING AGILITY

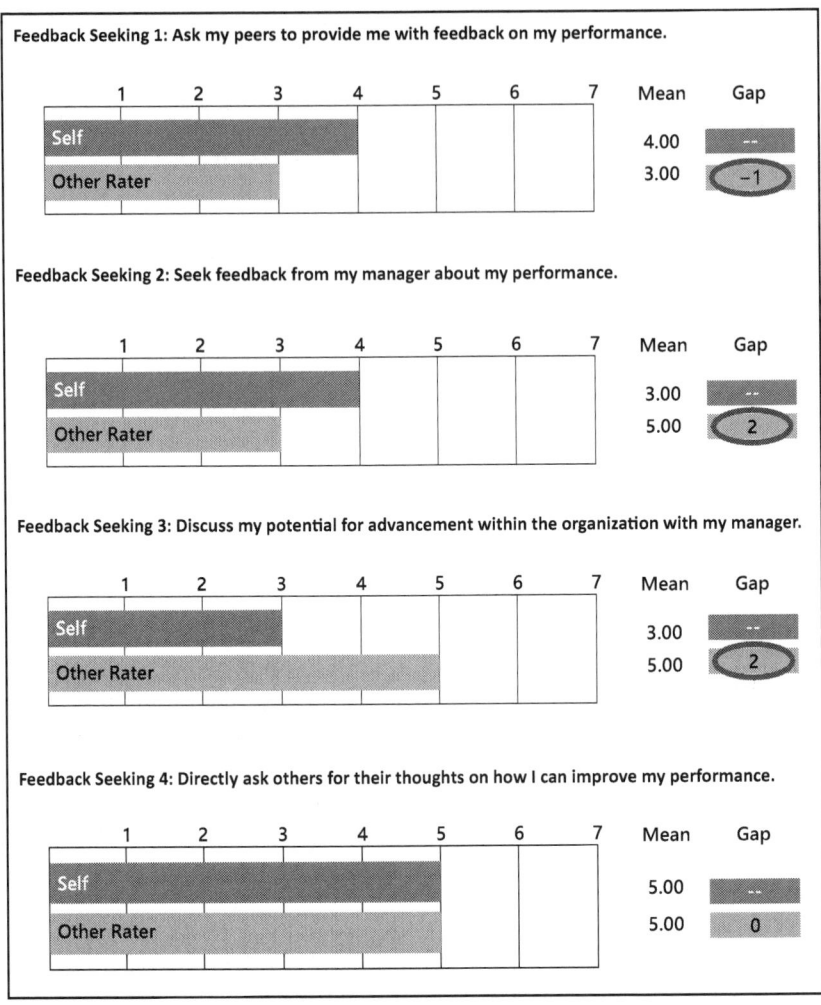

Burke 180: Dimension of Feedback Seeking with Self/Other Ratings for Four Items; Significant Differences Appear for Feedback Seeking Items 1, 2, and 3

BURKE LAS 360

When looking at item scores for the Burke LAS 360, the person being assessed may notice discrepancies at the rater group level. In the next example, in *Feedback Seeking* item 1, the manager, peers, and customers all rated the person lower than the person rated themselves. In *Feedback Seeking* item 2, the manager rated the person lower than they rated themself, but peers rated the person higher than the person rated themself. Those differences by perspective would be lost if the scores were averaged.

Feedback Seeking 1: Ask my peers to provide me with feedback on my performance.

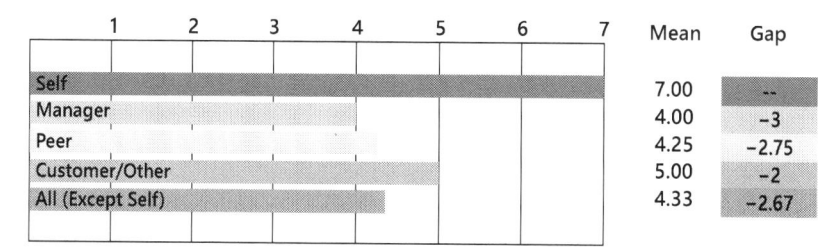

	Mean	Gap
Self	7.00	--
Manager	4.00	-3
Peer	4.25	-2.75
Customer/Other	5.00	-2
All (Except Self)	4.33	-2.67

Feedback Seeking 2: Seek feedback from my manager about my performance.

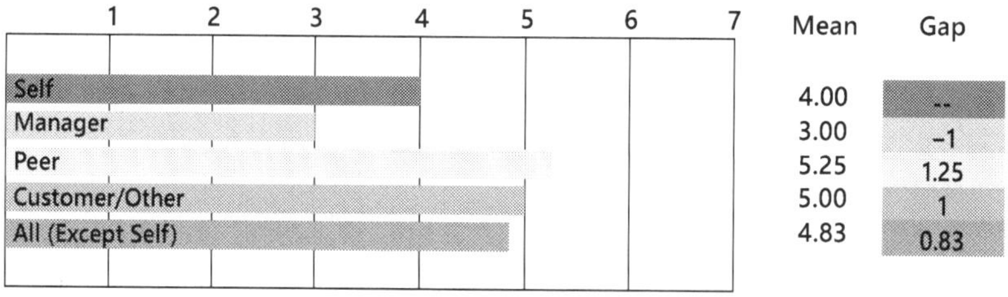

	Mean	Gap
Self	4.00	--
Manager	3.00	-1
Peer	5.25	1.25
Customer/Other	5.00	1
All (Except Self)	4.83	0.83

Feedback Seeking 3: Discuss my potential for advancement within the organization with my manager.

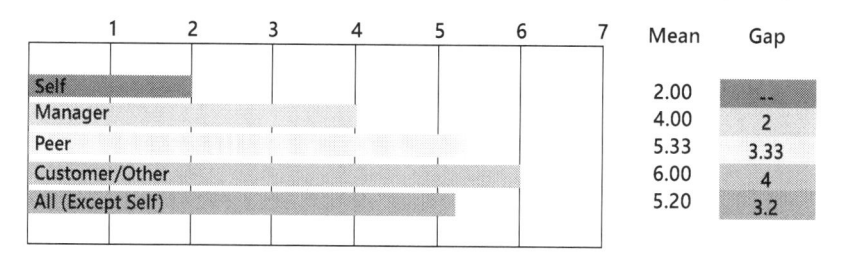

	Mean	Gap
Self	2.00	--
Manager	4.00	2
Peer	5.33	3.33
Customer/Other	6.00	4
All (Except Self)	5.20	3.2

Feedback Seeking 4: Directly ask others for their thoughts on how I can improve my performance.

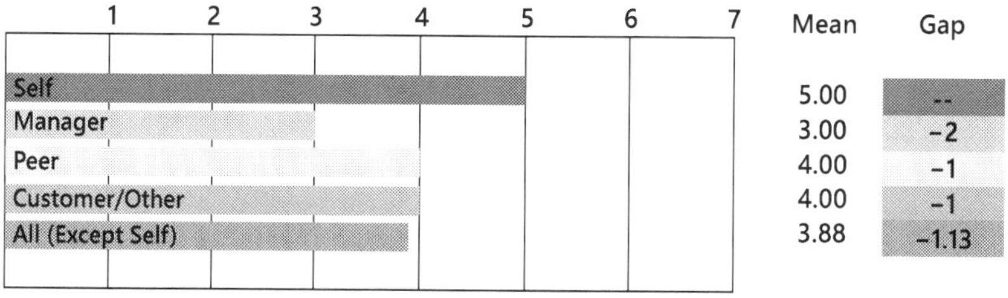

	Mean	Gap
Self	5.00	--
Manager	3.00	-2
Peer	4.00	-1
Customer/Other	4.00	-1
All (Except Self)	3.88	-1.13

Burke 360: Dimension of Feedback Seeking with Multiple Raters for Four Items

OPEN-ENDED QUESTIONS

There are two open-ended questions in both the Burke LAS 180 and 360 that ask the raters to provide specific examples for the person being assessed. Question 1 asks about strengths that the person should continue to make the most of. Question 2 asks about development opportunities. Assessment takers often find this section particularly helpful in clarifying some of the quantitative ratings. The comments are organized by rater category (e.g., self, manager, others).

- Question 1: What do you see as the greatest strength to leverage, and which actions should continue to be done?
- Question 2: What is their greatest opportunity for development?

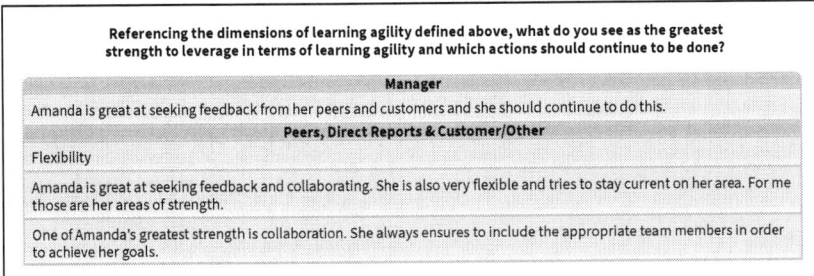

Summary Comments Regarding the Various Burke Assessments

The Burke LAS 360 version of the test is often used as part of a leadership development program to provide assessment takers with feedback on various areas of their leadership. The report may help them understand how the people with whom they interact may view their abilities, strengths, and weaknesses. Getting Burke LAS 360 results at the time of a promotion or a new assignment can be very timely and increase the likelihood of success.

We encourage participants to try to connect their responses to the open-ended questions to one or more learning agility dimensions. If the raters give a number of examples that all relate to a specific dimension, such as *Experimenting* or *Collaborating*, and those comments support the quantitative ratings, that is probably an important message for the assessment taker to consider.

Administratively, the multi-rater versions of the assessment are slightly more involved than the self-report versions. Sometimes those responsible for leader development or succession planning programs do not trust the self-awareness or objectivity of the participant and place value on the additional perspectives. (Note: Our data, to date [for the Burke Self-Report (LAI) Expanded Version (normed version)], have found a normal distribution of scores across all participants. This would seem to indicate that participants are not inflating their ratings.)

The Burke LAS 360 is everything you would expect from a full 360, with pages and pages of quantitative information across the range of perspectives. The qualitative data are rich and add clarity to the numerical ratings. This assessment is most often used in leader development programs, whether individually or programmatically focused.

When it comes to learning agility, the Burke Learning Agility Suite of products offers the customer a broad range of options. Work is currently being done on a team version of the Burke Learning Agility Inventory.

This chapter is intended to give leaders and coaches a more in-depth look at the features of each of the Burke assessments to determine which version is most appropriate for their application. The next chapter will exemplify how a coach might help an assessment taker (aka a leader) review and understand their Burke results.

CHAPTER 3

VALIDATING THE BURKE ASSESSMENT REPORT THROUGH DIRECTIVE AND NONDIRECTIVE COACHING

When it comes to providing feedback to the assessment taker regarding the Burke Learning Agility assessment results, E.A.S.I-Consult makes a distinction between "telling," or directive coaching, and "asking questions," or nondirective coaching. All Burke assessments require some interpretation of the results. A Coach helps the "leader" through his/her report and asks them questions about what they see in the data/information. They ask a lot of questions. Their role is not to be prescriptive, but to point out where there is a potential issue and ask the leader to tell the Coach what it means. That is why we use a gap between different raters of greater than 1 point as a potential issue. Let's say for example that there was a difference between how the leader rated themselves and how their boss rated them of 2 points. The Coach would say, that is a potential issue as the difference is greater than 1 point, specifically 2 points. What is that about? How do you explain the difference in ratings?

Working with senior leaders to understand and take action on their Burke assessment results often means the Coach needs to be directive with the leader. The Coach also needs to "validate" the assessment results with the leader. Validate means to help the leader understand and accept that the contrary information they are receiving is accurate. If the Coach is unable to confirm with the leader that this differences in ratings are accurate and signify a problem, then the leader is not likely to commit to the activities described in the development plan. End result is that nothing will change.

This generally means the coaching and questioning interaction is focused at the point of the development discussion. When a coach provides feedback on the different Burke assessment results/reports, a combination of asking and telling, relative to a person's assessment results, is most effective. I start by providing the assessment taker with some definitions of the terms I will be using. I define learning agility as "finding yourself in a situation where you have never been before, you do not know what to do, and you figure it out." I make a clear distinction between learning agility and learning ability, which is synonymous with cognitive ability or intellectual "horsepower."

As a coach, you should help the person who is receiving assessment feedback to appreciate the effect that "context," or environment, can have on learning agility. In addition, the feedback receiver should understand two other issues related to learning agility: skill and motivation. Skill is simply how proficient a person is in a learning agility area (either at the item level or the dimension level), and it tells the coach where to begin in terms of improving how well a person handles a first-time situation. There is no value placed on being skillful at something. Motivation involves how important learning agility is to the person receiving the feedback. If learning agility is not important to them, they are not likely to put energy into improving a capability.

Next, as a coach you should explain the organization of the assessment report. The self-report and the multi-rater report are organized somewhat differently, but both move from the highest-level perspective down to the item level. The multi-rater version includes written comments from assessors.

This foundational and definitional portion of the feedback is most effectively delivered using a directive approach. When moving into development, a nondirective or questioning style can be added.

Before you deliver the assessment taker's actual results, ask them to predict those results, but note that this can only be done *before* they receive their report. This is the only time you will receive their unguarded self-perception. Going forward, you as a coach might struggle with how the assessment taker "is" versus how they "see themself." Both perspectives can be inaccurate. Learning the assessment taker's unvarnished prediction upfront may provide insight into resistance you may experience from them with regard to their results.

The two versions of the Burke assessment (self-report and multi-rater) use different scales. The self-report version is normed, so the person is being compared to a larger population. (For more on this subject, read the Technical Report by Burke and Smith (2019).) The multi-rater versions use raw (actual) scores, and the person is being compared to their other raters.

Now for one other piece of context. There are three methods of getting information about people, and each has its strengths and flaws. The first is self-reporting, where you ask someone to predict their results. People know a lot about themselves, so this should be easy. The problem is that people cannot always be objective in their description of themselves.

A second source of information about someone is observation. In this instance, you would follow a person around and record everything they do. If you record only what you see, then you can create an objective description of what has occurred. That is the strength of this method. The flaw with observation is that you do not know what is going on in the person's head or why they are doing what they are doing.

The third method of obtaining information is to use an assessment, like the Burke LAI or LAS assessments. If the assessment effectively measures the concept you are studying, you should get an accurate result. (An assessment's technical report should provide information on how well the assessment is measuring the concept being studied.) A well-researched assessment should provide a good measure of that construct. If the assessment does not do a good job of measuring the construct that is being studied (validity and reliability), the results will not be particularly useful.

The best way to obtain information is to combine these three approaches to have convergence, overlap, or agreement on the information collected.

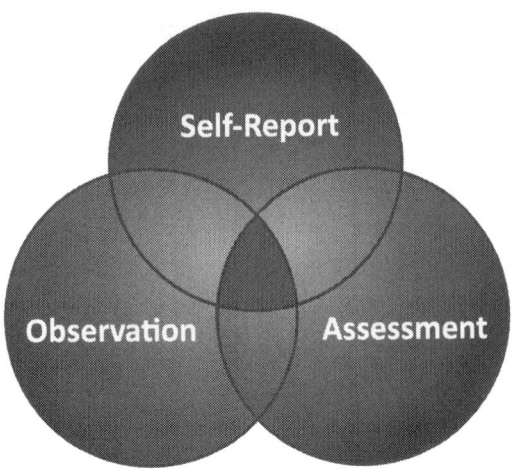

Back to the person's prediction of their results. For the Burke self-report, you as their coach can ask the person to predict whether they possess low, medium, or high learning agility. You then would ask them to predict their two highest-scoring and two lowest-scoring dimensions from the nine possibilities.

With the multi-rater version, there is not an overall score. Instead, the assessment taker's assessment by dimension is compared to a combination of all others who rated the person. A result is significant (meaning it warrants further attention) when the difference between the two perspectives on a dimension differs by a score of 1 or greater (remember that each assessor rates the person on a scale of 1 to 7).

If the predicted results are different from the actual report results, you want the person you are coaching to understand why. You may not resolve any differences for the overall score. For example, let's say that a leader predicted that their learning agility was going to come out as high. Technically, that would be above the 70th percentile. When the leader receives their results on the Burke Assessment the report shows (based on their item responses) them at the 40th percentile overall. Burke Assessment results at the 40th percentile is on the low side of medium and is a 30 percentile difference from their prediction. A coach would ask the person, how they would explain that difference? The leader may not have an answer. This is what is meant by not resolving those differences in scores, at least immediately. The coach could suggest that this difference be put aside and they look at the report by dimensions to better understand the feedback.

You can then look at the person's predictions for the two highest- and lowest-scoring dimensions. I have seen everything from 100% agreement on the two highest- and lowest-scoring dimensions as compared to Burke results to 0% agreement. Your objective is to decrease the number of discrepancies between the prediction and the assessment report. It is important to note that anyone using the Burke assessment must use the dimension definitions as written in these discussions. The person you are assessing needs to be clear that the definition of *Flexibility* in the Burke assessments is "Being open to new ideas and proposing new solutions." Using the definition as written may help resolve differences between prediction and assessment results. As the coach, you may need to get further into the report, down to the item level, before you can understand differences and what needs to be focused on for improvement.

When using the multi-rater version of the assessment, the overall score describes the assessment taker versus all others combined. Having the definitions of the dimensions available may be helpful. You can learn additional information from the different perspectives (e.g., self, boss, peers, and direct reports). Keep in mind that the definition of a "significant" difference in score is when the self-rating and another rating differ by 1.0 or more points.

As a coach, you need to indicate to the assessment taker that the next step is to look at their item scores by dimension. Looking at the Burke self-assessment first, each of the nine dimensions appears on a separate page in the report. The *Speed* and *Flexibility* dimensions have five bulleted items; the other seven dimensions have four items per page. Each item refers to a separate question on the assessment. The items use qualifiers such as "always," "sometimes," and "occasionally." If an item is a strength as the person rated it, it is a behavior or capability that the person always does or does often. If the report narrative uses qualifiers like sometimes or occasionally, then this is a capability the person can strengthen.

You can work with the assessment taker to identify specific examples that have posed problems in the past and what could have been done differently for the outcome to have been more positive or for the person to have been more effective. The discussion would then shift to a future situation requiring this capability and how to approach it so there will be a positive result. If the assessment taker needs improvement in several of the 38 items, you should limit the number of items discussed. Ask the person to make notes about all areas that need to be addressed. In our training sessions, we provide a learning journal for people to capture all areas needing further attention. Typically, it is best to limit this initial discussion to three, four, or five of the most significant opportunities, as this makes it more manageable. The additional report information can be used for future development or coaching sessions.

ABOUT THE MULTI-RATER BURKE ASSESSMENTS

The same process can be used for the multi-rater assessments as I described for the self-report version. The fact that there are more perspectives involved adds complexity. In addition to resolving or validating differences between the person's self-perception and the assessment results, you must help them resolve the differences between their own ratings and those of other rater groups (e.g., boss, peers, and direct reports).

It is conceivable that all rater groups assess a dimension or item as needing improvement. It is equally possible that the boss sees a dimension or item as a strength but another rater group (e.g., peers and direct reports) sees it as an area that needs improvement. Whatever the potential differences in perspective, if you are a coach, it is your role to help the learner understand the data. That may involve asking the learner to give specific examples to support their rating and helping the learner make connections. In some instances, you will need to have an opinion. If you disagree with the learner's interpretation, you should tell them, but support your assertions with data. An opinion without data or specific examples is just an opinion.

There are also sections of the multi-rater reports that include aggregated items that are based on how high or low the learner rated themselves compared to the other raters. These categories of items often show patterns. As a coach, you need to point out these patterns and the learner needs to speak to the implications.

The multi-rater reports include two open-ended questions that may provide additional data that support the numerical ratings. As the coach, you can "code" or identify if a qualitative comment is an example of a specific dimension (e.g., *Interpersonal Risk Taking* or *Reflecting*). Identifying and pointing out patterns is another option you can use to prepare the learner to act on the assessment report information.

The objective of this chapter was to describe a process for understanding and reviewing the assessment results. The remainder of the book will look at specific ways to develop each of the learning agility behaviors, with a chapter for each of the nine dimensions.

As a leader (assessment taker), you should read the chapters from the perspective of how you can approach your own development. As a coach, you can read the chapters and use the suggestions directly with your leader or supervisor. You can also use the suggestions as "thought starters" to develop your own approach to a learner's development.

CHAPTER 4

RICK CROSON: A LIFE EXAMPLE OF LEARNING AGILITY IN ACTION*

---

*Codes located in the margins of the following pages denote the learning agility dimension and item that Captain Rick was demonstrating. Their definitions are listed in the Glossary found on page 42.

At Burke LAI and Burke LAS presentations, my colleagues and I are frequently asked, "Is someone born learning agile, or can it be developed?" We believe learning agility can be developed; otherwise, we would not have gotten involved with the creation of an assessment to measure it. We also believe that assessments such as the Burke LAI, Burke LAS 180, and Burke LAS 360 give assessment takers a baseline that then allows them to focus more deeply in an area and determine which of the 38 items they need to strengthen. Another way to describe the baseline, or starting point, is skill level. Some part of "skill" may be genetically determined. We acknowledge that not everyone has the same learning agility starting point. Another factor described in learning agility presentations is motivation, or "How driven are you to put yourself in new and unfamiliar situations where you are going to look awkward and, on many occasions, fail at what you are trying to do?" People who are high in learning agility thrive on being in unchartered waters; others don't.

The idea of "unchartered waters" is a good segue to a case study of someone who exemplifies learning agility: Captain Rick Croson. Rick is a charter boat captain who runs out of Wilmington, North Carolina. He has been making a living on the water since he was 15 years old; he was 43 when this chapter was written. Rick grew up in the northern Outer Banks of North Carolina. The Outer Banks are often described as the "sport fishing mecca" of the East Coast. Almost every day at 4 a.m., 40- to 50-foot fishing boats take four to six fishers out of the treacherous Oregon Inlet for a day of fishing. The captain pilots the boat, negotiating the shoals in the inlet out to the Gulf Stream where the big sport fish reside. The captain mostly keeps to himself all day up on the bridge, with periodic but brief exchanges between the captain on the bridge and the mate on the deck to coordinate the fishing plan. On the 2-hour trip out to the Gulf Stream, the mate spends time readying poles, tackle, and bait to be put in the water once the fishing area is reached. A boat may have six to 12 lines in the water at any one point.

As any fisher will tell you, there is a difference between fishing and catching. The job of the captain and the mate is to get the boat to a spot where there are fish. It is then up to the fisher, once a fish is hooked, to get the fish to the boat, so the mate can gaff (using an iron pole with a hook on the end) and boat the fish. The captain and the mate work together to reduce the speed of the boat, and the mate gets other lines out of the way of the person fighting the fish. Typically, the fisher uses a fighting chair while reeling in the fish. Boating the fish, depending on its size and species, can take 20 to 30 minutes. Many fishers are novices and need a lot of direction, while others have a lot of experience and need little help. Most mates can gauge a fisher's experience level quickly. S1

Most of the people who go out on a charter boat do so to catch fish and have an enjoyable and exhausting day, but some on the boat are there because someone else asked them to come. Once the boat leaves the dock, everyone must stay there until the boat returns, whether they want to or not. There also may be people for whom part of the charter boat experience involves consuming alcohol. Many people experience motion or sea sickness, and alcohol consumption can exacerbate the sickness, leading to nausea and vomiting. For many, there is no relief until they're back on dry land.

Here we switch to the role of a mate. The role of a mate on a charter boat is to oversee the fishing experience and all aspects of customer relations while on the boat. Mates earn money through tips from their customers. It is important to be attentive and responsive. If you see a mate who is 15 years old and the only mate on the boat, it is safe to say that this "kid" knows their stuff; otherwise, they would not be there. In the Outer Banks, Rick became a mate at age 15 and continued in that role for 4 years. He earned his captain's license at age 18. This required him to demonstrate on-the-water knowledge and seamanship. Rick then found a boat in need of a captain and worked for 4 years as the captain of that boat until he moved to Wilmington, North Carolina. Rick moved to Wilmington, a well-known fishing area, to attend college, but stayed because of a girlfriend who later became his wife. F3 S5/IRT1

In Wilmington, Rick worked at a local fishing tackle store called Tex's Tackle and Bait for about 5 1/2 years. When he wasn't in the store, he was running charters as a captain-for-hire, in which he would go out on a customer's boat and take them fishing for the day. Rick told me that one of IG1

R2 the things that he learned as a captain-for-hire is that not everyone maintains their boats the way he maintains his. He also told me that he sunk two boats in the first year as a captain-for-hire. The lesson he learned?
R3 Never take out a boat before inspecting it. Some boat owners had issues with leaks or engine problems, and learning about those issues 10 miles
R2 out to sea was a problem. Captaining different people's boats exposed him
IG3/F2 to a lot of design features and boat types, some of which he liked and some of which he did not. During this time, Rick's experience at Tex's Tackle and Bait taught him about live and artificial bait and what worked, when
IG1 and where, and why.

BUILDING THE PERFECT LURE

I had the opportunity to go out on a fishing trip on the Gulf Stream with Rick. Once out on the water, he rigged some unusual looking lures on the lines, and we started catching fish one after the other. On the way back to the dock I asked Rick about the lures, as I had never seen any like them before. Here is the learning agility story he told me.

Rick had been forced into the use of lures in 2006 and 2007, when the federal government required the use of circle hooks, which changed how fish were hooked. During this time, Rick was captaining for people in major fishing tournaments that offered $50,000 to $1,000,000 prizes. Up to this point Rick had primarily fished with live bait.

One of his customers sent him to Hawaii for a week to fish with Captain Gene Vanderhoek, the most renowned lure fisher in the world, to increase his knowledge about using lures. Each day, Rick and Vanderhoek went out fishing. Their overall objective was to be sure that the lure they were using mimicked live bait. The captain showed Rick
E2 how to put each lure in a specific spot in the water and taught him some
C1/C2 tricks of making turns and how that changes the way the lure looks in the water. Rick sat next to Vanderhoek all week, constantly asking him
IRT2 questions. Rick would say to him, "Tell me what's going on," and the
C1/IG4 captain would share some of his tricks and other things he wouldn't give up. Vanderhoek used a bullet lure, which made a sharp entry into the water and had no action. Rick thought the captain wanted the lure

to skip occasionally, but Vanderhoek was looking at the lure to make sure it wasn't rotating.

Rick's experience in Hawaii taught him that each lure performs in a unique way and performance will be affected by weather and water conditions. By observing and talking to Vanderhoek, Rick learned the placement of different lures and how to get lures to perform a certain way in the water. Back in Wilmington, Rick practiced with lures to discover how weight and speed affected them. He determined how a boat's speed and shape affect lures and how to use weight to counteract the action of the water. He didn't just learn about lures—he studied to become an expert about them.

Rick also has experience using poppers, a type of lure that floats on the surface of the water and "pops" or jumps like live bait when a fisher tugs the line. He set a goal of designing a lure with neutral buoyancy so it would stay on the surface of the water. He worked with different materials and shapes, finally settling on balsa wood to make a tube body shaped like a flying fish. A bubble in the tube allowed it to move like a popper. It didn't take Rick long to realize that when he stopped the boat to fight a fish caught on his lure, his other lines also got hits. Pretty soon Rick was catching more fish when he was stopped than when he was trolling.

Rick began to make quick progress with his lure designs. He created seven different lures and immediately tweaked any designs that didn't work, viewing those adjustments as learning experiences, not failures. He kept a record of every change he made to the lures, and when a specific design worked, he replicated it. If he found a design he really liked, he made a mold, and 3D-scanned his original models.

He also played with colors and light, comparing the weights of resins and studying how some chemicals glowed under UV light. He learned about the UV spectrum, which is visible to some species of fish, by watching videos and talking to his diving buddies. Rick also figured out that lures that appeared purple above the water looked black at pressures below 100 feet of water, a realization that changed everything for him. In his search to improve his lures, he remade his resins, adding colors from the UV and color spectrum. There is no lure on the market that's made of the same resin material as Rick's, because he can make a lure buoyant and add color to it.

But were his lures a commercial success? Not exactly. The tackle store where he was selling the lures went out of business. It took him 2 years to figure out how to produce the product. In his second year, he was still making modifications. But the people who tested his lures began talking about how many fish they caught.

For Rick, crafting the perfect lure was about more than catching coolers full of fish. This, to him, is more important than how much money he would make. Rick does believe there is an economic case for using lures instead of artificial bait. A 12-pack of bait costs $18, compared to $25 for a single lure. However, a person can go through seven bags of bait in a day at a cost of $200. Rick believes fishers should not be dependent on one way to catch fish.

There was also an educational component to Rick's efforts. He delivered seminars at one-day fishing schools throughout the East Coast. He created his own charts to illustrate such specific scenarios as "at this distance and this angle, splash, splash, catch a fish," or "watch what happens when I put the rig back a little further in the water," or "this is not like using a ballyhoo." His audiences became convinced of Rick's views, and Rick enjoyed the opportunity to articulate what he learned in the process of creating lures.

BUILDING THE PERFECT BOAT

What follows is another story that Rick told me about trying to create "the perfect boat." There are so many variables to consider: the shape of the hull. How far is the boat above the water line? What type of engines, inboard or outboard? The fishability of the boat? Do you want to be able to walk around the boat and be able to fish from any location on the boat? Whatever you decide will impact how much space you have in the cabin. Where is all the equipment located? Some equipment are things like fish holders. Do you have a fighting chair? These are all questions without a right or wrong answer, but whatever you decide will have implications for the fishability of your boat.

A captain's boat is his office on the water; it is where they spend 200+ days a year and 12+ hours a day. Finding a boat that has all the elements you need to accomplish your mission is a never-ending quest. Rick, early in his fishing career in Cape Hatteras, bought a 20-foot boat for live-bait fishing and worked with the builder to design his ideal live-bait well tank. They used computer-aided design (CAD) to create a live-bait tank and then installed it on the boat to see how it would perform. It was a success.

Next, they broadened their thinking and began to envision a design for the ideal live-bait fishing boat. It would need to make it easy to catch live bait, travel in big sea conditions, go fast when the sea is calm, and travel efficiently in long-distance runs. It would also need to be transported on a trailer. They began by creating a set of specifications, and fished on boats with some of these capabilities. They identified elements they didn't like and used the CAD system to modify those elements.

The boat was initially "built" using CAD. The program showed the water line at a certain level, so they drew a line on the boat where that would theoretically appear. When the boat was put in the water, the drawn line and the actual water line were one and the same. Success. That boat, which was 27 feet long and had a 23-foot water line, was twice national champion and won more than 25 tournaments.

OPPORTUNISTICALLY RESPONDING TO NEW MARKET DEMANDS

You might expect that this success would turn Rick's focus from lures to building boats. But this is where his story takes another turn. His boat-building endeavor was put on hold when the nature of Rick's business changed almost overnight. A group of Japanese fishers who had found his website asked if they could hire him for a week of vertical jigging for amberjack in the Gulf Stream. The group was attracted to North Carolina and its reputation for plentiful, 100-pound amberjack. Rick was not familiar with jig fishing, which allows four fishers to fish at the same time on the same side of the boat, by angling the boat in the direction of the current. Rick learned this technique quickly, and took the group on the jigging trip. To his astonishment, the group caught not only amberjack, but also tuna, mahi, sailfish, wahoo, and grouper, species that swim at different depths in the water column. In a week's time, Rick lost interest in inshore Spanish mackerel fishing, his previous focus, and became entranced with this new endeavor, jig fishing.

Recognizing a new opportunity, Rick started advertising jigging trips on his website. He had interest from groups from Japan, China, Australia, Brazil, Vietnam, and Germany, as well as the U.S. West and Gulf Coasts.

Many of these new customers did not speak English. To "tell" them the depth to fish, Rick used colored fishing line to designate different depths. "If you go down four colors, you won't catch grouper," he'd explain to the fishers. As he told me, "My job was to put people on fish. My old approach had been trolling. With this approach you move rapidly across the fish. With jigging I would pull up to a spot, get the boat diagonal to the current and just drift." This method allowed the fishers to fish the same spot for an extended period. He estimated that the efficiency of this approach was 95% compared to 50% for trolling. The next revelation Rick had was the rods these new customers used. They were more parabolic. "I had been thinking about making a different type of fishing rod than what was being used in the United States and this is when that creative process began for me." Rick went through several versions of his shorter rods. I actually used an early version of his rod and it malfunctioned. He made some changes and was able to produce a well-functioning version of this rod that was effective in deep sea, jig fishing situations.

Rick found that after he had taken a few different groups jig fishing, he knew what to do to help improve their jigging technique. When these groups jigged, they jigged fast and had to stop and take breaks. At those points, Rick would throw a line in the water and show them how to pop, pop, pop, although most wouldn't try what he showed them.

CONTINUING TO LEARN AND GROW

For several years, Rick booked trips to the Gulf Stream for 185 to 190 days a year. His foreign business remained strong until exchange rates began to affect the ability of overseas customers to travel to the

United States to fish. His foreign business, when it started to decline, went away as fast as it had arrived, dropping from 190 days of bookings per year to just 40. His work as an instructor at fishing schools in the winter sustained him, but just barely. During this time, Rick lost the ability to advertise through his website. Rick's website "went down" and it needed to be revised to work effectively. He used this problem as an opportunity to "reinvent" who his customers would be and the types of fish he would target. The website would change what he advertised as the seasons of the year changed. F2

Rick used this lull to reflect on everything he had experienced during those extremely busy years to better understand the trajectory of his business. He knew he needed to recreate and update his website and organize the information to cater to different groups. He decided to offer Gulf Stream trips in the fall and spring. In the summer, his business would focus on inshore fishing for families and emphasize the "best experience" instead of catching the biggest or the most fish. R2/IG4   F5

Rick also remained open to new opportunities to learn and grow. He was hired by a customer who was visiting the United States from China and wanted Rick to take him fishing several times over a week. Slowly, the customer began to open up, as he realized Rick was not solely interested in his money. Rick eventually learned the man wanted to start a luxury boat business in China, which would be the first of its kind. He struck an agreement with Rick to help him as a consultant. The customer's factory will be in China, final assembly will be completed in Canada, and the boats will be sold in the United States, Canada, and China. Rick knows nothing about the process except for ship building, but, as with all exceptionally learning agile people, he will figure it out. F5   C2   S3/PRT1

GLOSSARY

Flexibility	**Being open to new ideas and proposing new solutions.**
F1	Flexibility 1: Propose solutions that others see as innovative.
F2	Flexibility 2: Consider many different options before taking action.
F3	Flexibility 3: Switch between different tasks/jobs as needed.
F4	Flexibility 4: Find common themes among opposing points of view.
F5	Flexibility 5: Articulate seemingly competing ideas or perspectives.
Speed	**Acting on ideas quickly so that those not working are discarded and other possibilities are accelerated.**
S1	Speed 1: Quickly develop solutions to problems.
S2	Speed 2: Get up to speed quickly on new tasks or projects.
S3	Speed 3: Readily grasp new ideas or concepts.
S4	Speed 4: Acquire new skills and knowledge rapidly.
S5	Speed 5: React well to unexpected problems.
Experimenting	**Trying out new behaviors (i.e., approaches, ideas) to determine what is effective.**
E1	Experimenting 1: Evaluate new techniques or different ways of solving problems.
E2	Experimenting 2: Experiment with unproven ideas by testing them out.
E3	Experimenting 3: Try different approaches to see which one generates the best results.
E4	Experimenting 4: Jump into action and learn by trial and error.
Performance Risk Taking	**Seeking new activities (i.e., tasks, assignments, roles) that provide opportunities to be challenged.**
PRT1	Performance Risk Taking 1: Take on new roles or assignments that are challenging.
PRT2	Performance Risk Taking 2: Engage in tasks that are ambiguous in terms of how to succeed.
PRT3	Performance Risk Taking 3: Embrace work that is risky, even if the outcomes are uncertain.
PRT4	Performance Risk Taking 4: Volunteer for assignments or projects that involve the possibility of failure.
Interpersonal Risk Taking	**Discussing differences with others in ways that lead to learning and change.**
IRT1	Interpersonal Risk Taking 1: Bring up problems and tough issues with others.
IRT2	Interpersonal Risk Taking 2: Ask others for help when needed.

IRT3	Interpersonal Risk Taking 3: Discuss my mistakes with others.
IRT4	Interpersonal Risk Taking 4: Challenge others' ideas and opinions even when they are shared by many people.
Collaborating	**Finding ways to work with others that generate unique opportunities for learning.**
C1	Collaborating 1: Look for ways to leverage the unique skills, knowledge, and talents of others.
C2	Collaborating 2: Work with colleagues from different backgrounds or job functions to share perspectives.
C3	Collaborating 3: Collaborate with people in other parts of the organization.
C4	Collaborating 4: Ask a variety of stakeholders for their points of view.
Information Gathering	**Using various methods to remain current in one's area of expertise.**
IG1	Information Gathering 1: Seek new information on topics related to my job or field.
IG2	Information Gathering 2: Update my knowledge and expertise through formal training or education.
IG3	Information Gathering 3: Read trade journals, newspaper articles, books, or other sources to stay informed.
IG4	Information Gathering 4: Collect data to increase my knowledge, evaluate my progress, and inform my next steps.
Feedback Seeking	**Asking others for feedback on one's ideas and overall performance.**
FS1	Feedback Seeking 1: Ask my peers to provide me with feedback on my performance.
FS2	Feedback Seeking 2: Seek feedback from my manager about my performance.
FS3	Feedback Seeking 3: Discuss my potential for advancement within the organization with my manager.
FS4	Feedback Seeking 4: Directly ask others for their thoughts on how I can improve my performance.
Reflecting	**Slowing down to evaluate one's own performance in order to be more effective.**
R1	Reflecting 1: Reflect on work processes and projects
R2	Reflecting 2: Take time to reflect on how to be more effective.
R3	Reflecting 3: Consider the reasons for and consequences of my actions or recent events.
R4	Reflecting 4: Critically evaluate work-related events with others in order to understand what happened.

CHAPTER 5

THEORY AND RESEARCH ON LEARNING AGILITY[1]

INTRODUCTION

Our interest in learning agility grew from a more general pursuit of understanding leadership and a long-standing concern about leader effectiveness. Initially, our focus was, and still is, learning agility in the context of leadership. Psychologists, especially I-O and organizational psychologists, have been interested in leadership, theoretically and empirically, for a long time—at least a century if we consider our predecessors who were involved in providing criteria for selection of U.S. military leaders for World War I. However, our track record toward a deep and clear understanding of, and predictive ability about who is likely to be an effective leader, has been less than ideal. According to a report by Hogan, Hogan, & Kaiser (2009), the failure rate (e.g., not accomplishing the goals for which one is responsible) of individuals in positions of leadership ranges from 30% to 67%, or an average of about one out of every two people in positions of leadership. Regarding leadership effectiveness, then, do we have a selection problem, or is the problem one of development? The answer is "yes"—that is, yes to both.

---

[1] We would like to thank Lauren Catenacci-Francois, PhD, and Jeanie Kim, PhD for their help in composing this chapter.

CURRENT LANDSCAPE OF LEADER SELECTION AND DEVELOPMENT

Another problem of leader selection worth mentioning is the notion of "implicit theory" (Hogan, Curphy, & Hogan, 1994). Many of us carry around in our heads an image of what a successful leader is supposed to look like, be like, and act like, such as tall, visionary, and authentic. But one person's list of leadership qualities and characteristics is rarely if ever the same as another's. The implicit theory idea helps to explain why search committees often have such a difficult time agreeing on a candidate: Each committee member has a different "leadership theory." Moreover, one possible consequence of the subjectivity in how individuals select leaders is the tendency to select people like oneself, which inherently favors men since many of the decision makers in leadership positions tend to be men. This preference for male leadership has likely contributed to the lack of gender representation in leadership positions.

Other potential problems of leader selection include (1) the lack of an agreed-upon set of general criteria that might include such qualities as self-awareness, energy level, cognitive complexity, and emotional intelligence; (2) the context and culture of the organization for the potential leader; and (3) the need for clarity regarding the goals the potential leader is expected to accomplish. Even when these problems have been addressed, it may not influence leader effectiveness. Moreover, we are experiencing today an ever-increasing rate of change and complexity. To do well, particularly in one's work life, learning and applying that learning as soon as possible is becoming more and more important. Thus, selecting potential leaders according to their ability to learn and agility at decision making as well as additional related actions.

With respect to issues of leader development, McCall (2010) makes the point that "to the extent leadership is learned, it is learned through experience" (p. 3). Job rotation can be a primary vehicle for this learning since having different experiences and responsibilities over time creates richer opportunities for learning than does staying in the same job for many years. This form of development is practiced religiously by the

U.S. Army. Soldiers, especially officers, rotate assignments about every 2 years. Moving from a command responsibility to a staff job and vice versa is routine—but learning from these new experiences is not routine. Unless one associates or connects the new experience with a thought, a cognition, an idea, or a concept, what one retains is perhaps no more than a story that one can tell, and not something that was learned and retained to be applied to similar situations in the future. To ensure that this reflection and connection occurs, feedback and coaching from others can be helpful (Seifert, Yukl, & McDonald, 2003; Smither, London, Flautt, Vargas, & Kucine, 2003). Finally, leaders should learn and develop certain skills that are critical to effectiveness, such as presentation and public speaking skills, managing conflict and negotiation skills, and interpersonal empathy skills.

These types of leadership development, which can be divided into the three categories of job rotation, reflection, and skills, are not proportionally equal. McCall (2010) refers to the 70-20-10 rule of leader development: In terms of contribution to the whole of development, 70% should be devoted to different job experiences; 20% to reflection, optimally with help from others, peers and coaches, for example; and 10% to learning new skills.

To summarize, leaders and potential leaders tend to grow and develop via the accumulation of challenging experiences (McCall, Lombardo, & Morrison, 1988; McCauley, Ruderman, Ohlott, & Morrow, 1994), and individuals vary in their ability to learn from such experiences (R. F. Morrison & Branter, 1992). However, finding organizations that practice the 70-20-10 rule, even with evidence to support the rule, is no easy matter. As McCall (2010) laments, even though there is evidence to support the importance of job rotation with assignments that are challenging and require new learning "on the run," getting executive decision makers to subscribe to this form of development as opposed to their preference for results and performance over learning is like asking for the impossible. But asking for the impossible may be a bit more possible with the help of learning agility. In other words, demonstrating that some people can learn more quickly and effectively than others and therefore apply this new learning and leadership capacities more efficiently (i.e., flexibly and quickly) could influence decision makers in an organization to support learning just as much as performance.

DEVELOPING THE MEASURE TO THE BURKE LEARNING AGILITY ASSESSMENTS

We concentrated on three areas from the literature that would provide direction for the content and substance of our behavioral statements for measurement. The first was experiential learning based on Training-Group (T-Group) theory and the laboratory method, which emphasizes learning how to learn (Bradford, Gibb, & Benne, 1964). The second area was behaviorism based on stimulus-response connections, early on by the likes of E. L. Thorndike (1908) and later by B. F. Skinner (1953). The third area was the work of Chris Argyris and his colleague, Donald Schön, covering such ideas as single-loop compared with double-loop learning, the importance of reflection, and defensive reactions (Argyris, 1985; Argyris & Schön, 1996; Schön, 1983). Our approach was to examine these theories for relevant concepts and ideas that would generate potential items for measurement.

T-GROUP THEORY

Also referred to as sensitivity training and the laboratory method, this body of learning theory and application evolved from Kurt Lewin's original work on group dynamics. There are at least seven goals of the laboratory method: (1) increased self-awareness; (2) increased ability to perceive and learn from the consequences of one's actions by paying attention to feelings, both one's own and others'; (3) clarifying and developing one's personal values and goals that are consistent with a democratic and scientific approach to problem solving; (4) increased consistency between one's beliefs and values with the requirements of a given situation; (5) achievement of behavioral effectiveness in transactions with one's environment; (6) applying new learning to new situations; and (7) learning how to learn by being an analyst of one's own ways of learning and developing abilities by taking initiative in seeking and using the resources of others and reciprocally becoming a resource to others (Bradford, Gibb & Benne, 1964). Methods for achieving these goals include (a) creating a climate of permissiveness, psychological safety, and inquiry; (b) establishing collaborative relationships for learning; (c) collecting data for analysis; (d) developing conceptual models or "maps" for understanding and organizing experiences; and (e) experimenting with new behaviors. Although T-Group theory and the laboratory method are oriented toward enhancing one's social and emotional intelligence, it is easy to see how this body of knowledge and practice provides a rich source of ideas for generating items for measuring learning agility in such areas as self-awareness, inquisitiveness, feedback seeking, action consequences, collaborating, feelings/emotions, and experimenting.

BEHAVIORISM

We were clear from the outset of our work on attempting to measure learning agility that two broad choices of what to measure were behavior and cognition. We deliberately chose the behavioral route. This choice was based on both parsimony and our background. In other words, measuring behavior seemed easier, at least comparatively speaking, than assessing how people think, and our collective graduate education has been more behavioral than cognitive. Thus, the second body of literature for direction of content for measurable items was behaviorism, that is, "changes in the form or frequency of observable behavior" (Brown & Sitzman, 2011, p. 472), more specifically, the stimulus-response connection. If a response is followed by some positive reinforcement of the response, the connection is more likely to remain for future use and application. To explain this stimulus-response connection further, Skinner used the term "operant behavior," which consists of (1) the behavior itself, (2) the antecedents of the behavior, for example, work unit climate or goal clarity, and (3) the consequences of the behavior, such as receiving positive recognition, improved job performance, and/or increased job satisfaction.

According to Brown and Sitzman (2011), "The primary focus of the behaviorist perspective is on the environment and the learning conditions it presents" (p. 472). They raise the important question of whether stimuli provide opportunities to seek environments where permission to experiment and take on challenging assignments can occur if not encouraged to learn appropriate responses. Should the appropriate response by the learner occur—the stimulus-response connection—followed by a positive outcome, Skinner's operant behavior, then learning is likely as a result.

Perhaps the most applied version of behaviorism is behavior modification. Applied appropriately, behavior modification can have a positive impact on task performance (Stajkovic & Luthans, 1997). It is assumed that learning as a consequence does indeed occur.

Our intent with the behaviorist perspective, therefore, was to create measurement items that would help the learner to seek environments where experimentation and taking on challenging assignments can occur even if not condoned, where seeking information as a means to broaden one's level of understanding is highly encouraged, where seeking feedback regarding whether the correct response is being practiced is encouraged, and where making mistakes leads to different responses and flexibility rather than to despair and giving up.

DOUBLE-LOOP LEARNING AND REFLECTION

Single-loop learning is knowing how to fix a problem but not learning anything new in the process, such as understanding the norms and values associated with the problem that support the probability that the problem will occur again. If the problem reoccurs, while one can fix it again, it means that causal factors (and double loop; Argyris & Schön, 1996) regarding the problem have not been addressed. At its simplest, single-loop learning is like fixing a leaky pipe with duct tape rather than replacing the pipe. For a more complex example, consider an executive in a business-industrial corporation facing a persistent problem of sinking productivity in their division of the company. Attempting to deal with the problem, the executive might conduct multiple meetings with their managers, exploring such areas as morale, technological glitches, reward system, and job satisfaction, to try to locate the source of the problem. With no resulting improvements or change of any kind, however, it may be that the executive is the source of the problem, for example, by not creating a safe working environment for the meetings so that difficult topics, or "undiscussables," can be freely discussed. It may be the case that the managers have been colluding with one another to avoid talking about uncomfortable issues; further, the managers may feel that their respective work performances are being unfairly evaluated and disagree with the executive's belief that competition among them is good for performance. But the executive would not learn about this conflict of beliefs unless they changed the norms and values of openness for discussion and solving problems. In other words, the real issue was the norm of how to behave in meetings, not job satisfaction or a technical problem. Changing the norm would create a different mode of inquiry and new opportunities for learning at another level. This next level of learning is the double loop—learning a new way of working together in addition to just fixing a problem (the single loop).

In addition to his work with Argyris (Argyris & Schön, 1996) on single- and double-loop learning, Shön devoted much of his work to developing an epistemology of practice (Schön, 1983). The epistemology of the academic world concerns the production (research) and distribution (education) of fundamental knowledge in general, but practitioners who attempt to apply this knowledge often have a difficult time of it. The divide between academia and the "real world" of practice that Schön addressed in the early 1980s continues today. Schön developed intellectual rigor in understanding competent practice by studying certain practitioners, architects, psychotherapists, engineers, planners, and managers. He began his work with the assumption that "competent practitioners usually know more than they can say" (Schön, 1983, pp. vii). Much of what practitioners know is tacit. The work that became known as reflective practice and reflection-in-action was an attempt to make what was tacit more explicit, understandable, and operable. As a practitioner, one's knowing is in one's action. The reflective practitioner, then, is one who can think in parallel forms—noticing what one is doing and at the same time discerning the setting, the context, within which one is acting and how the two (doing and discerning the setting) are interacting. This form of learning helps one to know what is repeatable, what seems to work and what doesn't.

For example, Schön (1983) describes a case of a psychotherapist in training and under supervision who is stuck regarding a patient's problem. After considerable exchange between the therapist and their supervisor, a hypothesis they explore is that the therapist's experience with their supervisor is a mirror of the experience of getting nowhere with the patient. The reflection-in-action leads to learning for the therapist in training.

This body of reflection-in-action, referred to as "knowledge-in-action" by Schön (1983), therefore provides a rich source of potential behaviors to apply to the agile learner and relates closely with the dimensions of interpersonal risk taking, performance risk taking dealing with complexity, openness, surfacing "undiscussables," and, of course, reflecting.

Finally, the work of Argyris (1985) on defensive routines provides considerable examples of what not to do when attempting to become more agile as a learner. Defensive routines are self-protective behaviors that we human beings use to prevent such feelings as embarrassment, fear, incompetence, anger, and resentment. These feelings block genuine discourse between and among people in organizations and lead to actions (and inactions) having nothing to do with solving real problems that exist in organizations and perhaps have existed for a very long time. Moreover, these defensive routines not only block solving the real problem but also inhibit learning. It is therefore the inhibition of learning that demands our attention. Behaviors associated with performance risk taking and interpersonal risk taking can help to break through defensive routines.

The last relevant component is speed, which is critical to this construct by definition. DeRue and colleagues (2012a; 2012b) explain that learning agility is about acquiring new information and integrating experiences quickly. Thus, speed is critical to learning agility because it differentiates those who are highly learning agile from those who are not.

By way of summary and clarification of the final theoretical process refer to Table 1. The table displays the main conceptual categories

TABLE 1

Dimension Name	Dimension Definition
Feedback Seeking*	Asking others for their impressions about your work performance; asking questions during the course of a task to make sure you are on track.
Information Seeking	Regularly reading relevant publications such as newspapers, magazines, professional journals; attending professional conferences and networking meetings; joining professional list serves.
Performance Risk Taking	Taking on job tasks or assignments that are difficult and challenging; volunteering for projects that have a possibility of failing; trying something new or unknown that would be highly rewarding if successful.
Interpersonal Risk Taking	Making oneself vulnerable by asking for help, admitting mistakes, pointing out the errors of others or having difficult conversations where "face" is at risk.
Collaborating	Regularly working with others to gain a different perspective on a task; creating interdependent work projects; asking for input from others in order to cooperate on tasks.
Experimenting*	Testing ideas and monitoring progress by collecting and reviewing data relevant to the task at hand; trying new things to see if they work; comparing different approaches to find the best one.
Reflecting*	Taking time to consider the work that has taken place and the assumptions in play as to what has gone well and what has not either alone or in a collective; reviewing events after they have occurred to consider how things can be done in the future.
Flexibility*	Moving fluidly between perspectives by recognizing when a mindset or belief should be abandoned for a new one; changing positions rather than becoming stuck; rejecting what has worked in the past in order to find what will work best in the future; maintaining a perspective on the environment in order to know when the context has changed.
Speed*	Quickly gaining an understanding of a new situation and the variables at play; correcting course by knowing when something is working and when it is not; being able to gain necessary new knowledge, skills, or abilities expediently.

for the three theories considered most relevant to measuring learning agility. In other words, these conceptual categories were the ones most representative of the theories and suitable for using a Likert scale format. Statistical analysis of actual ratings (correlating each item with each other and a total score rating) would then determine a working list. The conceptual categories in the table meeting the statistical criteria are denoted with an asterisk.

STAGE 1: ITEM GENERATION AND REDUCTION

For each of the nine dimensions (see Table 2) of the Learning Agility Inventory (LAI), the aforementioned literature was used to come up with five to six items according to the dimension's definition. Items were written to specify distinct but related behaviors that are observable demonstrations of the dimension according to its definition. Where applicable, we adapted items from the literature that have been shown to demonstrate the dimension of interest (e.g., *Feedback Seeking*).

This initial pool of items was tested in two samples, a convenience sample of online respondents and a sample of working professionals. As a result, the literature was revisited to clarify further the conceptual constructs. The items were reorganized into nine conceptual categories and new items were written to address any gaps in content. In total, four to five items were included for each construct after the research team wrote and discussed each item as demonstrating a behavior that fit the definition

TABLE 2: MEANS (M), STANDARD DEVIATIONS (SD), AND RELIABILITY STATISTICS

	Study 1 Psychometric Structure & Reliability N=393			Study 2 Convergent & Discriminant Validity N=199			Study 3 Criterion-Related Validity N=229		
	M	SD	α	M	SD	α	M	SD	α
Feedback Seeking	4.75	1.54	.87	4.87	1.06	.92	4.91	.96	.72
Information Seeking	5.55	1.60	.81	4.65	1.52	.90	5.41	.97	.72
Performance Risk Taking	4.93	1.46	.88	4.26	1.32	.89	5.42	.98	.76
Interpersonal Risk Taking	5.31	1.29	.78	4.44	1.12	.76	5.38	.76	.57
Collaborating	5.44	1.35	.88	4.58	1.34	.85	5.97	.66	.71
Experimenting	4.90	1.42	.85	4.80	1.11	.84	5.04	.86	.71
Reflecting	5.01	1.45	.83	4.96	1.21	.88	5.58	.75	.72
Flexibility	5.24	1.17	.81	4.87	1.06	.81	5.65	.62	.55
Speed	5.64	1.13	.85	5.28	1.09	.90	5.68	.69	.76

of the construct. In the final version, 38 items were included, with four items for each of the learning behaviors and five items each for *Speed* and *Flexibility*. For each question, participants were asked how often they engage in the following behaviors at work. Responses were assessed on a 7-point scale (1 = not at all, 4 = occasionally, 7 = very frequently).

Reliability

The means, standard deviations, and Cronbach's alpha for each of the subscales are presented in Table 2. Each subscale demonstrated satisfactory reliability, with all subscales achieving a .70 reliability or higher. Therefore, all items and subscales were maintained in the overall measure of learning agility.

STAGE 2: PSYCHOMETRIC PROPERTIES OF THE LAI

After finding preliminary support for the underlying structure and reliability of the LAI, we then proceeded to demonstrate construct validity. An integral component of the validity process is to examine the extent to which the instrument measures the unique construct it purports to measure by establishing relationships with similar constructs (convergent validity) while also showing that the measure is different from other constructs (discriminant validity) (American Educational Research Association, American Psychological Association, & National Council on Measurement in Education, 2014).

Existing literature in combination with the DeRue et al. (2012a; 2012b) model guided our thinking about which constructs would either theoretically converge or discriminate from learning agility. Openness to experience, for example, has been shown to correlate strongly with seeking new experiences and introspection (DeRue et al., 2012a; McCrae, 2004). Given that learning agility requires an individual to not only welcome new experiences but also seek them out, it is purported that openness to experience and learning agility are positively related. According to Vandewalle and Cummings (1997), individuals either welcome new challenges to demonstrate their capabilities or view them as threats that could undermine their competence. The former approach is known as learning goal orientation, which is often linked to higher performance (Elliott & Dweck, 1988). Given that learning agility embodies a similar approach of emphasizing learning from experiences, we believe that individuals who are learning agile are more likely to operate under a learning goal orientation. Moreover, the ability to learn from one's experience reflects a person's ability to navigate and deal with the changing demands of one's job and involves not only the willingness to learn, but also resilience, particularly when faced with adversity or unexpected events. Therefore, people who are learning agile should also be resilient. As individuals engage in complex tasks and enter ambiguous situations, such as taking on a new job or assignment as a leader, those who have a certain level of comfort dealing with uncertainty will be able to thrive more than individuals who are less tolerant of ambiguity. Moreover, those who are learning agile are expected to engage in active experimentation as they move through their role, developing stronger mental models of leadership, a clear identity as a leader, as well as a strong sense of self-efficacy. Furthermore, individuals who seek to reflect on events, focusing on both successes and failures, tend to improve on learning and performance via an increase in self-efficacy. Learning agility also includes the ability to be mentally agile, which according to Lombardo & Eichinger (2000) entails comfort dealing with ambiguity as individuals navigate complex situations.

Sound construct validity relies on evidence of convergent validity, but also discriminant validity, that is, demonstrating that learning agility is unrelated to constructs that measure variables different from learning agility. Given that an important part of learning agility is the ability to actively integrate new information and unlearn problematic patterns in one's approach, those who are closed to feedback or new experiences (e.g., defensive, rigid) are not likely to be learning agile (Oreg, 2003). Additionally, part of the learning process is personal accountability for one's learning. Therefore, those who believe that their behavior is guided by external circumstances (i.e., external locus of control) are, for example, less likely to assume efforts to influence others, exhibit better interactive behaviors with others, and seek information and knowledge concerning their situation. Another behavior that we wanted to differentiate from learning agility was risk aversion, which describes the tendency to ignore or overlook new opportunities that may lead to success. We also wanted to differentiate learning agility from different patterns of resistance, such as reactance, which captures individuals' resistance to social influences, invasion of personal space, or withdrawal of one's freedom (Brehm, 1966).

To summarize, learning agility was expected to converge with openness to experience, learning goal orientation, ego resilience, self-efficacy, and tolerance for ambiguity. Weaker correlations indicative of discriminant validity were expected with cognitive rigidity, external locus of control, risk aversion, and reactance.

SAMPLE AND PROCEDURE

Prior to data collection, a power analysis revealed a sample of 160 participants was needed in order to detect an effect with 98% certainty. A convenience sample of $N = 247$ participants were recruited through Amazon Mechanical Turk (MTurk). Of the total, 48 participants were dropped because they did not pass the attention check, bringing the total sample to $N = 199$ (89 female, 110 male). On average, participants were 34.96 years old (SD = 9.58) and had approximately 13.87 years of work experience (SD = 9.53). More than half of the sample was White/Caucasian (75.9%) followed by 9.0% Black, 6.0% Hispanic, and 6.0% Asian. The majority of participants were employed (96.00%, $N = 191$) when the survey was administered.

This study was administered through MTurk. After providing informed consent, participants were randomly presented with the measures of learning agility, after which they completed the LAI. Following this, they answered demographic questions. The survey took approximately 20 minutes to complete, and each participant was paid $2.75.

MEASURES OF LEARNING AGILITY

We measured learning agility using the scale described in the previous study (α = .96). Alphas for each of the subscales appear in Table 5.

CONVERGENT MEASURES

To reiterate, we explored convergent validity with five constructs that we believed were similar to but distinct from learning agility.

- Openness to experience. We used the 10-item version of the Big 5 measurement on the International Personality Item Pool. Participants responded to items such as "I believe in the importance of art" and "I enjoy hearing new ideas" using a 7-point scale (1 = very inaccurate; 7 = very accurate). The Cronbach alpha for this measure was α = .85.
- Learning goal orientation. We used Vandewalle and Cumming's (1997) 5-item subscale measuring learning goal orientation from the overall 12-item goal orientation scale. Sample items included "I often look for opportunities to develop new skills and knowledge" and "For me, development of my work ability is important enough to take risks." Participants used a 7-point Likert scale (1 = strongly disagree; 7 = strongly agree). The Cronbach alpha for this measure was α = .93.
- Ego resilience. Block's 14-item measure was used to measure ego resilience. Participants responded to items, including "I am more curious than most people" and "I get over my anger at someone reasonably quickly," using a 4-point Likert scale (1 = does not apply at all; 7 = applies very strongly). The Cronbach alpha for this measure was α = .83.
- Self-efficacy. Self-efficacy was measured using Sherer, Maddus, Mercadante, Jacobs, and Rogers' 17-item self-efficacy scale. Sample items included "When I make plans, I am certain I can make them work" and "When I have something unpleasant to do, I stick to it until I finish it." Participants used a 7-point Likert scale (1 = strongly disagree; 7 = strongly agree). The Cronbach alpha for this measure was α = .95.

- Tolerance for ambiguity. Tolerance for ambiguity was measured using McClain's 13-item Ambiguity Tolerance Scale. Participants responded to items such as "I don't tolerate ambiguous situations well" and "I find it hard to make a choice when the outcome is uncertain" using a 7-point Likert scale (1 = strongly disagree; 7 = strongly agree). The Cronbach alpha for this measure was $\alpha = .71$.

DISCRIMINANT MEASURES

Constructs like defensiveness are often hard to measure given their susceptibility to social desirability bias; therefore, we decided to measure constructs that would serve as proxies to defensiveness.

- Cognitive rigidity. Cognitive rigidity was measured using the subscale of Oreg's Resistance to Change scale (Oreg, 2003). The 4-item subscale assessed the extent to which individuals are rigid in their beliefs and included items such as "My views are very consistent over time" and "I don't change my mind easily." Participants responded to a 6-item Likert scale (1 = strongly disagree; 6 = strongly agree). The Cronbach alpha for this measure was $\alpha = .82$.
- Locus of control. An individual's locus of control was measured using two subscales developed by Levenson that gauge an individual's belief in the extent to which they possess control of their fate. The 8-item subscale "locus of control: belief in powerful others" reflects the belief that one's fate is typically controlled by others. Sample items included "I feel like what happens in my life is mostly determined by powerful people" and "If important people were to decide they didn't like me, I probably wouldn't make many friends." The Cronbach alpha for this measure was $\alpha = .87$. The second subscale measuring an individual's belief that fate is controlled by chance consisted of 8 items, including "To a great extent, my life is controlled by accidental happenings" and "I have often found that what is going to happen will happen." Both scales used a 6-point Likert

scale (1 = strongly disagree; 6 = strongly agree). The Cronbach alpha for this measure was α = .87.

- Risk aversion. Aversion to risk was measured using Cable and Judge's 8-item risk aversion scale (Cable & Judge, 1994). Participants responded to items, including "I am not willing to take risks when choosing a job or a company to work for" and "I am a cautious person who generally avoids risks" using a 7-point Likert scale (1 = strongly disagree; 7 = strongly agree). The Cronbach alpha for this measure was α = .82.

- Reactance. We used Hong's 11-item scale to measure reactance. Sample items included "Regulations trigger a sense of resistance in me" and "I consider advice from others to be an intrusion." Participants responded to a 7-point Likert scale (1 = strongly disagree; 7 = strongly agree). The Cronbach alpha for this measure was α = .91.

ANALYTIC STRATEGY

High correlations between learning agility and selected concepts from the research literature are often indicative of convergent validity; thus, we first examined the zero-order correlations between the various scales (AERA, APA, & NCME, 2014). While there is no universally agreed-upon cutoff used in the field of social sciences, both high positive and high negative values tend to be interpreted as more evidence for convergent validity, whereas smaller positive or negative values tend to be viewed as evidence for discriminant validity (Ferris, Brown, Berry, & Lian, 2008; Lewis, 2003).

For discriminant validity, similar to our process for establishing convergent validity, we considered the correlations between learning agility and the constructs that were purported to be unrelated. A convergent factor analysis (CFA) was also conducted to further establish discriminant validity by assessing whether a single-factor model provided a better fit to the data than a two-factor model in assessing which learning agility and the other construct were entered as separate variables. More specifically, if the chi-square were significantly worse for the single-factor model than for the two-factor model, this would provide evidence that the proper way to model the scale items is loading the items on two separate latent factors. This result, if confirmed, would suggest that learning agility is distinguishable from the other construct (Anderson & Gerbing, 1988).

STAGE 2 RESULTS AND DISCUSSION
Convergent validity

Learning agility was compared to openness to experience, learning goal orientation, ego resilience, self-efficacy, and tolerance for ambiguity. As shown in Table 3, learning agility and all its subscales were significantly correlated with learning goal orientation ($r = .32 - .63$, $p < .01$) and ego resilience ($r = .41 - .60$, $p < .01$). Openness to experience also showed evidence of convergence with the overall learning agility score ($r = .34$, $p < .01$); in particular, among the learning agility dimensions, *Speed* ($r = .46$, $p < .01$) and *Flexibility* ($r = .38$, $p < .01$) showed the strongest correlations to openness. This is not surprising given that one of the components to being learning agile is to be able to get up to speed and apply learned skills in new situations while remaining flexible and adaptable to the changing environment (DeRue et al., 2012a; 2012b).

Discriminant validity

The learning agility measure was compared to four constructs: locus of control—belief in powerful others ($r = -.20$, $p < .01$) and locus of control—chance ($r = -.17$, $p < .05$); risk aversion ($r = -.30$, $p < .05$); cognitive rigidity ($r = -.06$, ns), and reactance ($r = -.03$, ns). As expected, overall learning agility score and the subscales had little to no correlations with the proposed constructs.

Again, a CFA was conducted to ensure that learning agility was separate from the four constructs with which it showed little to no correlation (reactance, risk aversion, locus of control, and cognitive rigidity). For all four constructs, a two-factor model provided a significantly better fit than did a one-factor model: reactance, $\Delta\chi^2$ (1, N = 199) = 1062.0; risk aversion $\Delta\chi^2$ (1, N = 199) = 481.3; locus of control–powerful others, $\Delta\chi^2$ (1, N = 199) = 590.8; locus of control–chance, $\Delta\chi^2$ (1, N = 199) = 562.9; and cognitive

TABLE 3: STAGE 2 DESCRIPTIVE STATISTICS AND CORRELATIONS (CONVERGENT AND DISCRIMINANT MEASURES)

	M	SD	1	2	3	4	5	6	7	8	9	10
1. S	5.27	1.09										
2. F	4.87	1.06	.60**									
3. IS	4.64	1.42	.51**	.54**								
4. C	4.58	1.34	.45**	.63**	.55**							
5. FS	4.17	1.52	.33**	.51**	.56**	.55**						
6. R	5.00	1.21	.58**	.70**	.62**	.60**	.51**					
7. E	4.79	1.11	.65**	.61**	.54**	.59**	.49**	.57**				
8. IRT	4.44	1.12	.43**	.60**	.46**	.58**	.66**	.53**	.55**			
9. PRT	4.26	1.32	.59**	.60**	.60**	.63**	.55**	.56**	.69**	.57**		
10. Overall LA	4.59	1.01	.67**	.74**	.77**	.78**	.83**	.77**	.77**	.77**	.81**	
11. LOCP	-.37	1.28	-.27**	-.12	-.18*	-.06	-.11	-.17*	-.21**	-.11	-.26**	-.20**
12. LOCC	-.86	1.29	-.25**	-.16*	-.11	-.11	-.08	-.17*	-.18*	-.16*	-.16*	-.17*
13. LGO	5.01	1.27	.63**	.49**	.44**	.42**	.32**	.46**	.57**	.38**	.57**	.57**
14. B5-O	5.20	1.13	.46**	.38**	.26**	.29**	.16*	.30**	.34**	.22**	.29**	.34**
15. TA	4.05	.73	.33**	.33**	.31**	.27**	.30**	.23**	.35**	.29**	.55**	.41**
16. GSE	5.13	1.15	.66**	.42**	.47**	.29**	.24**	.45**	.43**	.34**	.42**	.49**
17. RA	4.47	.87	-.23**	-.19**	-.25**	-.22**	-.19**	-.15**	-.27**	-.15*	-.50**	-.30**
18. RTC-CR	4.03	1.00	.12	-.03	.02	-.06	-.16*	.08	-.03	-.06	.13	-.06
19. RCT	3.67	1.27	-.10	-.06	-.04	-.00	-.03	-.03	.04	-.13	.06	-.03
20. ER	2.83	.48	.57**	.54**	.42**	.41**	.43**	.52**	.56**	.48**	.60**	.62**

*Significant at the p = .05 level. ** Significant at the p = .01 level.

Note: 1-9 are LAI subscales: 1. Speed; 2. Flexibility; 3. Information Seeking; 4. Collaboration; 5. Feedback Seeking; 6. Reflection; 7. Experimentation; 8. Interpersonal Risk Taking; 9. Performance Risk Taking; 10. Overall LA Score; 11. Locus of Control–Powerful Others (LOCP); 12. Locus of Control–Chance (LOCC); 13. Learning Goal Orientation (LGO); 14. Openness to Experience (B5-O); 15. Tolerance for Ambiguity (TA); 16. General Self-Efficacy (GSE); 17. Risk Aversion (RA); 18. Resistance to Change–Cognitive Rigidity (RTC-CR); 19. Reactance (RCT); 20. Ego Resilience (ER).

rigidity, $\Delta\chi^2$ (1, N = 199) = 286.2; all p values were less than .05. These results suggest that learning agility is a separate construct from reactance, risk aversion, locus of control, and cognitive rigidity.

In summary, the results presented in this study support the convergent and discriminant validity of the LAI, showing that learning agility is strongly related to learning goal orientation, openness to experience, tolerance for ambiguity, self-efficacy, and ego resilience, yet discriminant from external locus of control, risk aversion, cognitive rigidity, and psychological reactance.

STAGE 3: CRITERION-RELATED VALIDITY

After finding evidence to support that the LAI is a distinct construct, we sought to examine the criterion-related validity of the LAI to determine whether it predicts performance.

SAMPLE AND PROCEDURE

The sample for this study consisted of N = 229 (94 female, 135 male) high-potential employees participating in a leadership development program, Potential Leader Development Center (PLDC), at a large multinational food and beverage corporation located in the United States. The average age was 39.6. To participate, all participants had to have a minimum of 2 years of performance rating and have at least 2 years of tenure with the company. As part of the program, participants completed a battery of four assessments, which included the Raven's Progressive Matrices, Occupational Personality Questionnaire (OPQ-32), and a custom developed biodata inventory and situational judgment test. Of the 721 potential respondents, N = 229 volunteered to complete the LAI, which was administered during a post-assessment feedback survey 9 months after the completion of the program.

MEASURES
Learning agility

As with previous studies, learning agility was measured using the same 38-item instrument. The reliabilities for each of the nine dimensions/subscales had moderate to high internal consistency. See Table 4.

TABLE 4: CORRELATION OF LEARNING AGILITY AND PERFORMANCE RATINGS

	Mean	SD	Overall	1. FS***	2. IS	3. PRT	4. IRT	5. COL	6. EXP	7. REF	8. FLEX	9. SP
Age	37.66	8.00	-.15*	-.16*	-0.08	-.16*	-0.02	-0.13	-.16*	-0.08	-0.13	-.16*
Tenure (Years)	9.54	6.58	-0.11	-0.01	-.14*	-.15*	0.06	-0.10	-0.13	0.04	-0.07	-0.13
PLDC Score (Spearman's rho)	2.59	0.96	.35**	.31**	.16*	.35**	.15*	.34**	.37**	.19**	.21**	.27**
3-Year Perf Average	6.87	.058	0.12	0.11	0.07	.15*	0.06	0.03	0.11	0.08	0.06	0.12
2014 Perf Rating	6.77	0.84	0.06	0.03	0.07	0.06	0.07	-0.02	-0.02	0.0	0.08	0.13
2015 Perf Rating	7.08	0.87	0.08	0.10	0.08	0.08	0.01	0.04	0.07	0.04	0.04	0.06
2016 Perf Rating	6.80	0.88	0.09	0.06	0.02	.15*	0.05	0.04	0.13	0.06	0.03	0.08

$N = 214$, $*p < .05$, $**p < .01***$.
Note: 1–9 are LAI subscales: 1. Feedback Seeking; 2. Information Seeking; 3. Performance Risk Taking; 4. Interpersonal Risk Taking; 5. Collaborating; 6. Experimenting; 7. Reflecting; 8. Flexibility; 9. Speed.

PERFORMANCE

Performance data was captured using several methods. Job performance was measured using a 3-year average of job performance ratings, in addition to the overall PLDC performance as measured by a weighted average across the four different assessments. Individuals were also rated by their supervisors based on the company's leadership competency model known as the Leadership Excellence Framework (LEF), which focuses on key competencies composed of abilities such as demonstrating strategic and conceptual thinking, creating an inclusive culture, and collaborating across boundaries.

STAGE 3 RESULTS AND DISCUSSION

Prior to analyses, subscale scores were generated by computing the average of all items in the subscale. Additionally, we averaged all 38 items on the LAI to obtain an overall learning agility score.

Pearson correlation analyses were conducted to assess the relationship of the LAI to performance outcomes, as shown in Table 4. Given that the PLDC score was categorical and represented quartile scores, we used Spearman correlation to calculate the relationship between LAI and the PLDC score (Daniel, 1990). Results indicated that although overall learning agility was not correlated with any performance indicators, the *Performance Risk Taking* subscale had a significant positive correlation with the 3-year performance average ($r = .15$, $p < .05$). There was also a significant positive correlation between all of the learning agility subscales ($r = .15$ to $.37$, $p < .05$) as well as the overall learning agility score ($r = .35$, $p < .01$) and performance on the PLDC assessment suite.

The results from this stage provide evidence for predictive validity. Specifically, the LAI showed predictable relationships across the company's leadership competencies shown in Table 5. These results are desirable because many of the leadership competencies were theoretically aligned with the LAI dimension constructs. For example, significant positive correlations were found between the overall LAI and measures of strategic ability ($r = .24$), inspirational leadership ($r = .34$), talent management

TABLE 5: CORRELATION OF LEARNING AGILITY AND LEADERSHIP COMPETENCIES

	Mean	SD	Overall	1. FS***	2. IS	3. PRT	4. IRT	5. COL	6. EXP	7. REF	8. FLEX	9. SP
Judgment	0.45	0.23	.14*	0.03	0.07	0.11	0.12	.14*	.15*	0.09	.13*	.13*
Global Mindset	0.42	0.25	0.10	0.10	0.09	0.06	0.06	0.09	0.06	.15*	0.09	-0.01
Strategic Agility	0.42	0.23	.24**	.19**	0.13	.33**	.15*	.17*	.19**	0.06	.21**	.18**
Communication	0.33	0.23	0.08	.15*	0.06	.20**	-0.03	0.03	0.07	-0.05	0.03	0.05
Coalition Building	0.41	0.21	.17**	.27**	0.04	.20**	0.10	.20**	0.11	0.03	0.10	0.08
Inspirational Leadership	0.46	0.24	.34**	.40**	.22**	.39**	.15*	.27**	.23**	.18**	.22**	.18**
Talent Management	0.43	0.22	.21**	0.12	0.04	.23**	.22**	.21**	.22**	0.10	.16*	.15*
Integrity and Trust	0.86	0.17	-0.01	0.03	0.09	0.01	-0.13	-0.09	-0.01	-0.01	-0.04	0.01
Courage	0.48	0.16	-0.05	-0.02	-0.08	-0.08	-0.04	-0.06	-0.03	-0.01	-0.01	0.03
Intellectual Capacity	0.48	0.27	.15*	0.05	.14*	.18**	0.08	.14*	0.11	0.07	.15*	.14*
Stamina	0.43	0.22	0.09	0.11	-0.02	.24**	-0.08	-0.01	0.13	-0.01	0.07	0.11
Composure	0.42	0.24	0.02	0.07	-0.06	0.07	-0.02	0.04	-0.01	-0.03	0.03	0.06
Innovation	0.43	0.26	.22**	0.12	0.06	.32**	0.12	.19**	.21**	0.05	.22**	.20**
Execution Capability	0.48	0.20	0.01	-0.01	-0.01	0.08	-0.12	-0.02	0.02	-0.01	0.01	0.08
Learning Agility	0.43	0.18	.17*	.13*	0.10	.23**	0.04	.13*	.16*	0.07	.16*	0.10

$n = 229$, * $p < .05$, ** $p < .0$.

Note: 1–9 are LAI subscales: 1. Feedback Seeking; 2. Information Seeking; 3. Performance Risk Taking; 4. Interpersonal Risk Taking; 5. Collaborating; 6. Experimenting; 7. Reflecting; 8. Flexibility; 9. Speed.

(r = .21), intellectual capacity (r = .15), and judgment (r = .14). All LAI subscales were significantly positively correlated with measures of leadership (r = .15 to .40, p < .05). LAI scores predicted coalition building (r = .17), which makes sense given its similarity to the collaboration subdimension of the LAI. Additionally, the leadership competencies such as inspirational leadership, talent management, and judgment involve different components of learning agility such as being willing to experiment and take risks while taking in relevant information in order to make informed decisions.

GENERAL DISCUSSION

Our motivation for this developmental research on an instrument to assess learning agility came from frustration about the process of selecting people for leadership. The track record of individuals in positions of leadership is not exactly impressive. On average, the failure rate, based on measures of goal accomplishment, is around 50% (Kaiser, Hogan, & Craig, 2008). In other words, there is something not quite right about the criteria we use for selection (e.g., technical competence is no guarantee for success as a leader). About a decade ago we had read that something called learning agility might be a strong predictor of success as a leader, a captivating idea. On further investigation, however, we were not satisfied with the measures of learning agility at that time, as they focused too much on cognitions and attitudes rather than observable behaviors. Thus began the long journey of developing a measure of our own. With the three studies reported here and three doctoral dissertations later (Smith, 2015; Drinka, 2018; Catenacci-Francois, 2018), we are farther down the road. Even though we have a long road yet to travel, we are encouraged by the results so far. For example, in stage 3, all of the dimensions of the LAI showed a significant positive relationship with inspirational leadership (r = .34). Moreover, learning agility correlates positively with a number of other important leadership competencies across organizations such as learning goal orientation, tolerance of ambiguity, locus of control, strategic agility, innovation, talent management, and judgment.

With these promising findings, let us explore, at least to some extent, what the essence of our measure of learning agility means. According to our measure, learning agility:

1. Concerns both skill and motivation. Increasing one's learning agility is about developing certain skills, for example, how to work with others who have different backgrounds and points of view, or how to reflect about an experience one had and what it may mean. At the same time, one must have a desire to learn, to be curious about things and events, to want to accumulate knowledge even for the sake of simply enjoying knowing more today than one knew yesterday. The role model here is Leonardo da Vinci, perhaps the most curious and agile learner who ever lived (Isaacson, 2017).

2. Means being active rather than passive. In order to learn, or at least to learn effectively and speedily, one must do something—take a risk, volunteer for an ambiguous assignment, ask for feedback on one's performance, have a voice in meetings, etc. The learning comes from being mindful of the consequences of one's actions, how others react to one's acts, and whether the desired outcomes were actually realized.

3. Means, although not in every instance across the nine dimensions of the Learning Agility Inventory, more interpersonal actions are expected than solo activities. Being a loner can only take one so far in developing agility. Interacting with others is more dominant for learning agility—seeking feedback, collaborating, performance risk taking, and experimenting usually involves others.

4. Means having tolerance for ambiguity, that is, proceeding with actions even though one may be unsure about what to do. Acting will generate consequences that one can assess and decide whether to try again or to attempt something entirely new and different.

5. Involves, at least at times, taking a risk. In everyday parlance, it means "sticking your neck out." Risk taking also creates the conditions, at least potentially, for being embarrassed. Making mistakes, and perhaps being embarrassed, is part of the human condition.

The agile learner will look carefully at the possible causes of their mistake, put them in their "memory bank," and quickly move on and try something else to lessen the feelings of embarrassment as quickly as possible.

6. Requires courage. Courage is not one of the nine dimensions but undergirds many of them. Taking risks, seeking feedback, experimenting, and adapting to changing circumstances are acts of bravery.

These six meanings deepen our understanding of learning agility and what may be required to be considered an agile learner.

But the question remains of whether an agile learner outperforms others. We have a long way to go in attempting to answer this question. One study by Smith (2015) in one organization showed a relationship between overall learning agility and performance of hedge fund managers, a correlation of .43. In our stage 3, the overall learning agility rating was not positively correlated with job performance. However, one of the LAI dimensions, *Performance Risk Taking*, was significantly correlated with the company's 3-year performance average ($r = .15$). More interestingly, learning agility was strongly correlated with many of the company's leadership competencies, including inspirational leadership, talent management, strategic agility, judgment, and coalition building, most of which reflect various components of learning agility. For example, to be able to set a strategy and maintain sound judgment likely requires one to be flexible across situations, quickly developing solutions to problems and grasping new ideas and concepts, which are all hallmarks of a learning agile individual. Overall, those reporting high levels of learning agility seem to exhibit more skill with social aspects of the work environment while also having a keen eye toward the company's strategy and innovation. Thus, learning agile individuals are more likely to be oriented toward understanding how units and teams function and fit together, while possessing the collaboration skills to facilitate change.

Even though the measures of predictive validity are meager, there are indications that continuing to look for opportunities to measure LAI ratings with performance, regardless of how many different ways performance is defined, is worth pursuing.

LIMITATIONS

Even though there is now a version for multi-rater feedback, the LAI results reported in these three studies is based on self-report ratings. We know that self-reported assessments can be positively skewed. Even so, two points need to be made. First, the 38 items ask the respondent to answer "to what extent do you. . . ." It is easier for the respondent to provide a rating of how often they do a behavioral act than to, say, agree versus disagree with a statement. Second, we are finding that respondents tend to follow a normal distribution; see, for example, Smith's (2015) study.

We have yet to find a gender difference, but our data sets are too small to draw a definite conclusion. Stage 3 results showed a slight age difference (see Table 4), a negative correlation of −.15, indicating that perhaps learning agility wanes with age. These are correlations, so caution is in order regarding any conclusions. Our studies are "snapshots" preventing us from drawing any conclusions about learning agility and performance over time. Ideally, future research tracking performance and learning agility could correct this limitation (DeRue et al., 2012a; 2012b).

Although stage 3 was conducted with a large global corporation, the sample consisted of individual contributors with high potential, not experienced leaders. Also, we did not have contextual data such as types of roles and different departments. In another study, albeit limited in scope, we found that job level is significantly correlated with learning agility in that those who manage larger businesses, departments, and functions tend to be more learning agile than those who were in lower-level positions and roles (Burke, Roloff, Mitchinson, Catenacci, Drinka, & Kim, 2016).

IMPLICATIONS

As noted at the outset of this chapter, our curiosity about learning agility was a result of our longstanding interest in the study of and teaching of leadership in graduate courses and executive programs. Also, we were looking for ideas about how to do a better job of selecting people for positions of leadership and then developing them for the challenges they would face. Learning agility seemed to be a potential remedy, at least in part, for the selection problem since buried in the definition were criteria for being more effective at what to consider when selecting possible candidates: flexibility, risk taking, capable of getting up to speed quickly, collaborating, etc. And assuming further that learning agility is predictive of the successful execution of leadership, then the nine dimensions consisting of 38 items of behaviors in our assessment instrument provide a worthy list of specific developmental goals such as improving one's skills of seeking feedback, reflecting, and experimenting; see Hoff and Burke (2017) for suggestions regarding the development of these skills.

We believe that one can learn more about how to learn. The learning process consists of a set of skills that one can acquire. Yet we also believe that to be a more effective learner one must be motivated to want to learn more at a faster pace. The agile learner is both skilled and motivated and therefore better equipped to deal with a rapidly changing world. Organizational decision makers would do well to select agile learners for their organizations, especially for positions of leadership, and to provide and nurture a culture that supports risk taking with learning goals in mind, not just performance objectives.

CHAPTER 6

FLEXIBILITY

The Burke definition of the dimension of Flexibility *is "Being open to new ideas and proposing new solutions."*

In just about any unfamiliar situation, *Flexibility* is part of the solution. DeRue et al.'s original research on learning agility conducted in 2012 concluded that learning agility was solely about *Speed* and *Flexibility*. Burke, in 2016, confirmed these findings and identified seven other capabilities, or dimensions, that fully clarified learning agility.

Learning agility is measured by 38 questions. *Flexibility* constitutes five of those items. *Speed* also has five questions; all the other dimensions are measured by four questions. While no dimension is weighted more than others, by virtue of having five questions to measure it, *Flexibility* contributes more, statistically, to the overall score.

Burke's definition of *Flexibility* has two parts: "Being open to new ideas and proposing new solutions." Let us look at each part of that definition separately.

To increase the *Flexibility* dimension of your own learning agility, you need to determine *the level of openness to new ideas*, both your own and that of your organization. When describing the organization's openness to new ideas, we are talking about context. While this needs to be a consideration, we need to focus on what the individual can do to increase *Flexibility*.

If you are trying to broaden a person's perspective, you could examine a situation or scenario that they oppose. What must change for that scenario to be feasible? Perhaps some parts of the scenario have merit, but the person rejects the whole idea as presented. Demonstrating flexibility might mean looking at the parts deemed acceptable, then revising the unacceptable parts, to provide another option. It might include considering how many of those acceptable partial options could be revised, or combined with other partial solutions, to end up with additional choices.

The second part of the definition of *Flexibility* is "proposes new solutions." What needs to happen to maximize the number of available solutions? It sounds simple: just suggest several things that have not yet been mentioned. However, there could be limitations within the individual or the organizational environment that create restrictions. We focus initially on the individual. A technique used to expand options or solutions is "brainstorming." That requires everyone involved to suspend judgment for a period of time and generate as many ideas as possible. One idea can feed on another, and the more fun you have with ideas and each other, the greater the output.

In phase one of brainstorming, idea generation, the more suggestions, the better. In phase two, the ideas are evaluated against an identified criterion. In this step the list gets much smaller; sometimes ideas are combined. This is also where organizational constraints may be a consideration.

Idea generation will be less successful in phase one if the group evaluates ideas early on. Another issue that can limit creativity or the generation of solutions is the organization's environment. You may hear this referred to as the organization's culture, or, as you will hear some say, ". . . the way we do things here."

DeRue's conceptual model of learning agility identifies an element affecting the outcome as *context*. In my work with organizations, I cannot emphasize enough that *context matters*. A few quick examples:

- I worked at a 100-year-old manufacturing company. It was an unwritten norm that you could not state opinions or make suggestions until you had tenure in the organization. Most employees "grew up" in the company, so it was understood that it was best to keep your mouth shut. *How many new ideas were volunteered?* Very few.
- I worked at this same company in the days before PowerPoint. Presentations were put on acetates, and someone turned the acetates during your presentation. It was seen as "helpful" for audience members to find typos in the presenter's acetates. It felt like spotting typos was more important than the content itself. *How many new ideas came forward in that environment?* Not many.

What follows is a scale that can be used to determine the degree of openness in an organization and as a basis for understanding *Flexibility* in a specific situation. In this scale, a rating of 1 or 2 indicates it is "very difficult for new ideas to be accepted." A score of 6 or 7 says "this environment is very encouraging toward new ideas."

OPENNESS AND ACCEPTANCE SCALE: NEW IDEAS

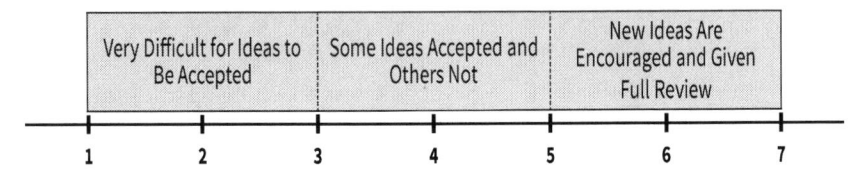

Very Difficult for Ideas to Be Accepted	Some Ideas Accepted and Others Not	New Ideas Are Encouraged and Given Full Review
1 2	3 4 5	6 7

Up to this point we have been describing *Flexibility* at the dimension level (open to new ideas and proposing solutions). A deeper look into *Flexibility* involves the five items or behavioral descriptions of *Flexibility*, which are the way it is measured in the assessment. Those descriptors are the following:

1. Proposes innovative solutions
2. Considers options before acting
3. Switches among different tasks/jobs
4. Finds common themes
5. Articulates competing ideas/perspectives

Let us examine these descriptors one by one, review how to assess current skill levels, and propose examples of what you can do to help someone become more capable in these areas.

Besides asking learners to assess their capability in each of the five descriptors of *Flexibility*, you also want them to assess their ability to transfer that skill to new and different situations. The first descriptor is *proposes innovative solutions*.

FLEXIBILITY DESCRIPTOR 1: PROPOSES SOLUTIONS THAT OTHERS SEE AS INNOVATIVE

There are many books on innovation, and it is not our intent to make someone an expert on innovation. But it is important to define it, at least according to some experts. Hopefully, that will help you find a way to measure a learner's starting point, and then give them ideas for how to improve.

This example comes from Nick Skillicorn, *What Is Innovation?* (2016). Skillicorn starts with his own definition of innovation and then asks four other "experts" to add theirs. Those definitions appear below.

- Skillicorn: Turning an idea into a solution that adds value from a customer's perspective.
- Kevin McFarthing: Introduction of new products and services that add value to the organization.
- Jeffrey Baumgartner: The implementation of creative ideas in order to generate value, usually through increased revenue, reduced prices, or both.
- Gijs van Wulfen: A feasible, relevant offering such as a product or service with a viable business model that is perceived as new and is adapted by customers.
- Jorge Barba: The future delivered.

We now have some descriptions of innovation. I will use these as an example of Burke's descriptor 1 (examples of innovative solutions). Next, I will identify common themes in those definitions (which is Burke's descriptor 4). First, I am going to identify the themes in the definitions.

Looking across Skillicorn and colleague's five definitions for innovation, there seem to be three clear themes. The main theme is in bold.

1. Theme 1 – Value. Experts state that the *solution must deliver value* (increased revenue, reduced price, or both).

2. Theme 2 – Customer. Experts state that there needs to be *an object of this innovation*: a customer (the organization).

3. Theme 3 – Solution. Experts concur that *ideas become solutions* (products or services).

These themes can be used to create scales. These scales will allow you to assess the degree of innovation by theme.

FLEXIBILITY DESCRIPTOR 1: SCALE TO MEASURE A SOLUTION'S INNOVATIVENESS

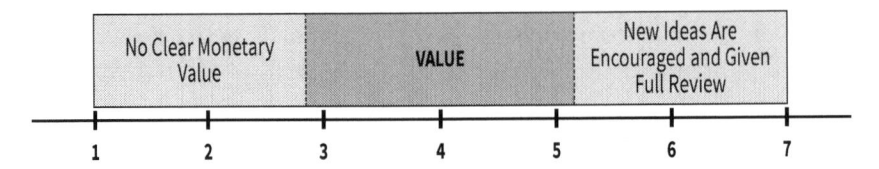

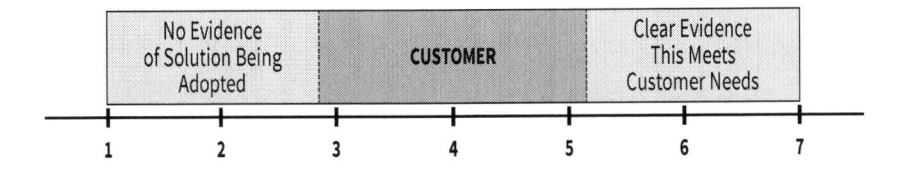

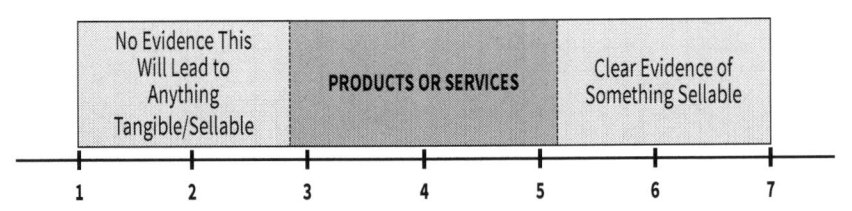

No Clear Monetary Value	VALUE	New Ideas Are Encouraged and Given Full Review

1   2   3   4   5   6   7

No Evidence of Solution Being Adopted	CUSTOMER	Clear Evidence This Meets Customer Needs

1   2   3   4   5   6   7

No Evidence This Will Lead to Anything Tangible/Sellable	PRODUCTS OR SERVICES	Clear Evidence of Something Sellable

1   2   3   4   5   6   7

Developing or Increasing a Person's Ability to Introduce Solutions That Are Innovative

Now you have a means to quantify a solution's innovativeness, using the scales just shown. The scales measure value, customer, and products or services, providing a way to calibrate a solution's innovativeness.

On this scale, being more innovative requires three things: increasing the value of ideas, focusing more on the customer, and linking ideas to products that are sellable. If someone has taken the Burke assessment, they would have their starting score on this item. As a coach or supervisor, you could work with the learner to select a project requiring innovation and set a goal to increase their score on each scale. With your assistance, the learner could incorporate the three elements described in the previous chart in their innovation plan. After reviewing the plan with you, the learner would execute the plan. At the midpoint of the project, you would meet with the learner to review their progress, make any needed course corrections, and outline steps to complete the plan. You would conduct an assessment at the end of the project to determine what went well and what could be improved. You would ask the learner questions such as, "Have your skills improved in this area? Can you measure and quantify that change?"

Now let us move on to the second descriptor of *Flexibility*, which is *considers options before acting*.

FLEXIBILITY DESCRIPTOR 2: CONSIDERS MANY DIFFERENT OPTIONS BEFORE TAKING ACTION

The definition of the *Flexibility* dimension is "Being open to new ideas and proposing new solutions." People who are open to new ideas and propose solutions consider their options *before* acting, in the context of a situation in which they have never been, don't know what to do, and need to try to figure it out. For many people, the initial inclination is to recall past experiences that resemble the current situation, then remember the solution they used previously and try to convince themselves that it will work again. While a solution that worked in the past might be appropriate and could be the one that ultimately works the best, it is worth considering and trying a few other approaches first.

First, generate as long a list as possible of potential ways to solve the problem. This is called inductive reasoning, and it requires you to open your thinking to as many possibilities as you can generate. It is a form of brainstorming.

Set a time limit for brainstorming. If brainstorming is the means being used to attack a problem, set a limit on the time spent generating solutions.

If you are doing this by yourself, it helps to know when to stop. Focusing on idea generation for a defined period allows thoughts to bubble to the surface after the initial flurry of ideas. When you stop prematurely, you prevent late suggestions from emerging.

Try not to evaluate ideas while generating them. Once you start to censor ideas, you are restricting rather than expanding your options. After the brainstormed list has been created, you can establish criteria to evaluate those ideas. The goal here is to broaden perspective by considering options before acting on a single idea.

Consider using a Force Field Analysis. This technique was created by Kurt Lewin in the 1940s. It requires you to describe the current problem/opportunity/situation. Your description defines the "current state" of the issue.

Lewin would have you draw a vertical line down the center of a page with your one-line problem description at the top. He indicated that there are forces that promote or try to move that current state forward and that there are an equal (or roughly equal) number of opposing forces that are working to prevent the situation from changing. In some cases, the promoting and the restraining forces are the opposite of one another.

Here is an example. A small organization is introducing a new technology and expects it to streamline operations. A promoting force could be the people in favor of it. A restraining force could be others who want to keep the current approach. There might be other promoting and restraining forces that impact the situation but that are not the exact opposite of one another.

In this example, another promoting force could be that the new technology will allow the company to enter a new line of business. A restraining force could be that existing labor contracts require the use of this old technology; switching to newer technology would require paying all affected employees until the contract expires. This would be an example of promoting and restraining forces that are not the opposite of one another.

This illustration shows how Lewin would define a problem and list all the promoting and restraining issues surrounding it.

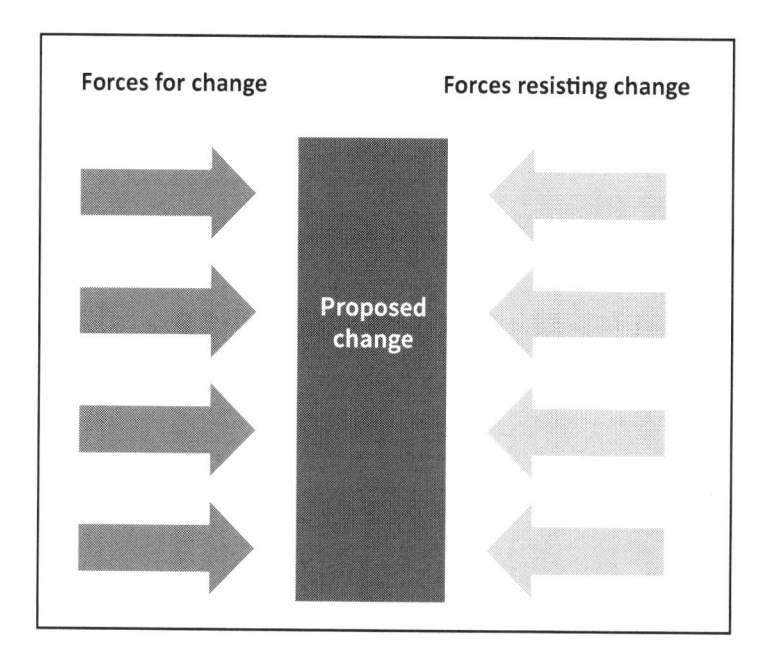

[Diagram: Forces for change (arrows pointing right) and Forces resisting change (arrows pointing left) converging on a central "Proposed change" box.]

Once an exhaustive list of the promoting and restraining forces has been created, you can assign a weight or a percentage to each force, identify ways to increase or decrease the weights of the promoters or restrainers, or combine forces identified on each side.

The next step in any process that generates ideas is to *consider options before acting*. Too often, people rush to a solution that they believe will solve a problem. One capability of more learning agile people is that they take time to consider all options before acting, which is *Flexibility* descriptor 2. People who are skilled in this dimension walk around the challenge and view it from several perspectives. Brainstorming and Force Field Analysis are two techniques that can allow people to increase their capability in the area of *Flexibility* descriptor 2. As with *Flexibility* descriptor 1, the learner must identify and follow a process to articulate and execute a plan. If you are a coach, your role is to help the learner stay on track and hold them accountable. Once the project has been completed, you and the learner should review any improvement in capability in this area and define a new project to continue to increase capability.

FLEXIBILITY DESCRIPTOR 3: SWITCHES BETWEEN DIFFERENT TASKS/JOBS AS NEEDED

Many of us would simply call this descriptor "multitasking." Like multitasking, switching among different tasks or job means doing more than one thing simultaneously and doing each one well.

Multitasking is something that takes practice, a fact I learned firsthand when I was selected to participate in a 2-year "high-potential" program. There were 20 of us in the program, and we met once a month on a development panel. Our work included screening issues that were scheduled to go before a strategy committee the following day.

The strategy committee met on a monthly basis to decide on a range of issues, all of which were vitally important to the company: new advertising campaigns, capital project requests, legal issues, status of labor negotiations, and proposed changes to company healthcare plans. The strategy committee's members received volumes of information, and the Management Development Panel were required to interpret and stake out a position on most issues. No one on the committee had expertise in every discipline discussed.

Those of us who were on the development panel had been identified as potential senior managers or general managers, roles that require taking in lots of information, developing frameworks to explain relationships, and forming opinions. In other words, these were roles that required learning agility.

The development panel was an exercise in developing skills associated with learning agility. At our Management Development Panel meetings, presenters shared their analysis of an issue and the proposed solution. If their proposed solution was not approved by the Management Development Panel, we gave them our feedback and told the presenters what issues needed to be addressed before presenting again. The next day, a subset of our panel would attend the strategy committee meeting to hear the same presentations for approval at that level. The company's CEO asked for the panel's position on each issue at the end of the presentations. Then the strategy committee discussed the presentation and made its own decision. The panel's input affected the outcome of the strategy committee's decision.

Now let us suppose you are a coach for an employee who is looking to improve their *Flexibility*. How could that person become involved in activities that require them to "switch among different tasks or jobs," thus requiring them to increase their learning agility? Here are some ideas:

1. Being assigned to a task force outside their area of expertise and being expected to contribute or even lead the group.
2. Serving on the board of a nonprofit, where they would actively participate and contribute, and maybe be assigned to a committee. Chairing a committee or taking an assignment outside an area of expertise would be even better.
3. Getting involved in a community organization or homeowners' or residents' association and seeking a leadership position.
4. Joining a team at work that is looking into acquisitions or business expansion. Participation would be based on their need for development in this area. You would put them in a role outside their comfort zone and expect them to contribute. You would rate the employee on their contribution.

If your employee had taken a Burke assessment, you would know their current capability as rated on a scale from 1 to 7. This is their baseline, and you could select a development assignment using those assessment results. You can adjust the degree of difficulty of the development assignment depending on the individual's needs. By establishing milestones and holding regular discussions with your employee, you can regularly measure their progress until the project is completed and you determine the next step for increasing capability.

FLEXIBILITY DESCRIPTOR 4: FIND COMMON THEMES AMONG DIFFERENT POINTS OF VIEW

The idea in finding common themes involves a thematic analysis of information. Earlier in this chapter, we described common themes as they related to different definitions of innovation. Here is Skillicorn's definition again, along with those of other experts:

- Skillicorn: Turning an idea into a solution that adds value from a customer's perspective.
- Kevin McFarland: Introduction of new products and services that add value to the organization.
- Jeffrey Baumgartner: The implementation of creative ideas in order to generate value usually through increased revenue, reduced prices, or both.
- Gijs van Wulfen: A feasible, relevant offering such as a product or service with a viable business model that is perceived as new and is adapted by customers.
- Jorge Barba: The future delivered.

THEMES

Looking across the five definitions, three themes emerge, which are in bold.

1. The *solution must deliver value* (increased revenue, reduced price, or both).
2. There needs to be *an object of this innovation*: a customer (the organization).
3. *Ideas become solutions* (products or services).

As a learner, one way you can develop the capability to find common themes is by analyzing written information. Finding similarities allows you to focus on the highest or lowest common denominator, identify patterns in a description of information, or focus on areas of agreement or disagreement.

Learning agility requires the ability to figure out what to do when you do not know what to do, and to find common themes to organize information and assemble a solution. It requires a willingness to ask questions: What was going on? Is there something about it that is similar to an earlier situation? How is this situation different?

Developing this capability begins with the assumption that everyone has the ability to find themes. If you are starting at the lowest level of this capability, you can begin by working on a thematic analysis of written content about a familiar topic, such as a sport, hobby, or area of interest. If you're working to develop this area, find a coach or accountability partner who will provide feedback and stretch your thinking.

Once you do this a few times and feel comfortable, pick some content out of your area of expertise or comfort zone and go through the same review process. To push yourself further, you can take on this role in a live discussion with your coach or partner observing. You should write down your observations and share them with your coach. For a final exam, you can complete a thematic analysis in real time during a discussion so that the coach can provide immediate feedback. You and your coach would rate how well the questions you asked moved the discussion forward or resolved an impasse. Based on both assessments, your coach would give you a project that requires you to perform at a higher level in this area.

FLEXIBILITY DESCRIPTOR 5: ARTICULATE SEEMINGLY COMPETING IDEAS OR PERSPECTIVES

The final item under the *Flexibility* dimension is being able to articulate competing ideas or perspectives. Many of us get locked into our own views on an issue. *Flexibility* as a dimension is focused on proposing new or competing ideas or perspectives.

One way to improve this capability is to state a position, then take the exact opposite stance and be able to defend or debate your position with someone on the other side of the issue. Success will be determined by an individual's ability to make a case for something contrary to their own, original position.

Put simply, a flexibly skilled learner can advocate and argue *both* sides of an issue, and specific points from either side, thereby making any position sound plausible.

Now we will look at this situation from the role of a coach. How well does your employee articulate competing ideas or perspectives? You would start with their Burke assessment score on this item. On a 1- to

7-point continuum, 1 is "unable to support their position on both sides of an issue" and 7 is "able to convince others about the merits of both sides of an issue with equal levels of persuasion." You would give the employee an issue and ask them to state their position. The employee would then be asked to return at a specific time and make as convincing a presentation as possible about the merits of the opposite position. You would then rate their convincingness on a scale of 1 to 7. You would talk about what went well and what is needed to improve in the stating of the opposite position. You would repeat this process with a new issue until you felt the employee had achieved a rating of 5 or 6 on the presentations. The exercise could then be expanded to a broader audience and a tougher issue and repeated until the employee is able to make a strong case on most sides of any issue.

A FEW FINAL THOUGHTS ON *FLEXIBILITY*

Developing *Flexibility* as a dimension of learning agility is difficult. Ultimately, *Flexibility* requires us to demonstrate creativity, inductive and deductive reasoning, thematic analysis, changing paradigms, multitasking, and *being open to new ideas and proposing new solutions*. It requires us to take actions that feel uncomfortable, such as becoming immersed in an unfamiliar culture, country, or function; searching for connections; taking performance risks (which while helpful as part of *Flexibility*, we will get into as a separate chapter on risk taking). Being willing to state a connection and be wrong is an element of *Flexibility*, even if it means you will be teased or mocked. *Flexibility* requires a willingness to forgo instant success for a series of small successes that will hopefully accumulate over time. Or as it is often said, a journey of 1,000 miles begins with a single step.

CHAPTER 7

SPEED

The Burke definition of the dimension of Speed *is "Acting on ideas quickly so that those that aren't working are discarded and other possibilities are accelerated."*

When my colleagues and I talk to groups about learning agility, there is a question that almost always is asked early in the discussion: Is the smartest person in the room the most learning agile? When we ask the group this question, the reaction is interesting. Most people give a somewhat qualified "No." When asked why, there's usually someone who will give an example of a person they know who is very "book smart" but lacks common sense. Others will describe a coworker who has a high IQ (intelligence quotient) but cannot apply their intelligence effectively.

In presentations to groups about learning agility, part of our discussion involves the difference between agility and ability. Ability is defined as cognitive ability. Agility is defined as being able to figure out what to do in a new or ambiguous situation. Cognitive ability is important to a point, but beyond that threshold it does not differentiate between people who are more learning agile and those who are less learning agile. Of the nine dimensions of learning agility, *Speed* is the one most connected to cognitive ability. However, unbridled cognitive ability can work at cross purposes with a person's learning agility. The behavioral descriptors associated with the *Speed* dimension are the following:

1. Quickly develops solutions
2. Gets up to speed on new tasks/projects
3. Readily grasps new ideas/concepts
4. Acquires new skills and knowledge rapidly
5. Reacts well to unexpected problems

This chapter will examine how to develop these behaviors. As context, we will introduce some of the ideas from Daniel Kahneman's 2011 book, *Thinking, Fast and Slow*. We will examine how behaviors from other learning agility dimensions are instrumental in developing the behaviors in the *Speed* dimension. As a reminder, *Speed* and *Flexibility* are the drivers of learning agility. Five of the 38 items on the Burke assessments involve the *Speed* dimension.

Before beginning work on increasing the behaviors associated with *Speed*, consider this caveat. Incorrect answers accomplished quickly are not what this dimension is about. In *Thinking, Fast and Slow* Kahneman introduces us to Systems 1 and 2. He describes them as imaginary characters that are involved in our responses to situations. System 1 is the fast thinker, the quality that most people associate with Burke's dimension of *Speed*. System 2 is the other voice, the one that slows things down and monitors the efforts of System 1 (Kahneman, 2011, p. 13). Both parts of Kahneman's response system possess strengths and shortcomings. We will delve into them to better understand their impact on *Speed* and its relation to learning agility.

One other concept that needs to be considered at the beginning of the discussion of Speed is the role of habits. Habit is an important element that affects Speed or interferes with how quickly and consciously someone does something. If you are trying to change some action and part of your response is habitual, it will interfere with making the change. The *Encyclopedia Britannica* defines a habit as any regular repeated behavior that requires little or no thought, is learned, and is not innate. Kashy, Wood, and Quinn (2002) determined that 45% of the actions people perform daily are not actually decisions, but habits (p. 198). So since habits in large part are unconscious, they need to be identified and made explicit to understand how they may or may not be affecting Speed.

For Burke, *Speed* means a combination of fast and correct in execution. Kahneman captures this dichotomy in the conclusion of his book: "The acquisition of skill requires a regular environment, an adequate opportunity to practice and rapid and unequivocal feedback about the correctness of thought and actions" (p. 416). Notice that Kahneman uses the word "environment"; for our purposes, we would use "context" (p. 416). The passage cited also alludes to other Burke LAI dimensions, but we will deal with those later in the chapter.

In this passage, Kahneman goes on to say, "When these conditions are fulfilled, skill eventually develops and the intuitive judgements and choices that quickly come to mind will mostly be accurate. All this is the work of System 1 which means it occurs automatically and fast. A marker of skilled performance is the ability to deal with vast amounts of information swiftly and efficiently" (p. 416). (What Kahneman is describing involves part of the first four Burke behaviors under *Speed*. He puts more emphasis on behaviors three and four.)

Kahneman continues, with paraphrasing noted by ellipses: "What happens in the absence of skill? System 2 must be called in . . . When System 1 is searching for an answer to one question it simultaneously generates the answers to related questions, and it may substitute a response that more easily comes to mind for the one that was requested . . . The heuristic (rule of thumb) answer is not necessarily simpler or more frugal than the original question – it is more accessible, computed more quickly and easily. The heuristic answers are not random, and they are often approximately correct. And sometimes they are quite wrong. System 1 . . . Does not generate a warning signal when it becomes unreliable . . . There is no simple way for System 2 to distinguish between a skilled and a heuristic response. Its only recourse is to slow down and attempt to construct an answer on its own, which it is reluctant to do because it is indolent . . . What can be done about biases? . . . little can be achieved without a considerable investment of effort . . . System 1 is not readily educable" (pp. 416–417).

Kahneman says he has improved only in his ability to recognize situations in which errors are likely. "The decision could change if the problem is reframed. [This is what Burke's *Flexibility* dimension focuses on.] . . . I [Kahneman] have made more progress in recognizing errors of others than my own. The way to block errors in System 1 is simple in principle; recognize the signs that you are in a cognitive minefield, slow down and ask for reinforcements from System 2" (p. 417).

In Part 3 of Kahneman's book, he describes some additional cautions about things that impede our ability to get to the correct answer: "Difficulties of statistical thinking. The limitations of our own mind, our excessive confidence in what we believe we know, our inability to acknowledge the full extent of our ignorance and uncertainty of the world. We underestimate the role of chance in events" (pp. 199–265).

In Part 5, he tells of the experiencing self and the remembering self. System 1 handles the automatic formation of memories and its rules. When people choose what memories to repeat, they are guided by their remembering self (pp. 391–397).

Many enthusiasts of learning agility believe that *Speed* is innate and closely linked to cognitive ability. They would likely argue that *Speed* is about genetics and cannot be developed. Kahneman has written an entire book about thinking fast, which focuses on the things that can interfere with our ability to get to a correct answer quickly. We all have blind spots, Kahneman says, and it is better to address those biases at the beginning than to defend flawed thinking after the fact. Habits are triggered by cues (context) and do not require supporting goals or conscious intensions. While someone is speeding along in System 1, these habits that have been honed support unconscious activity toward a familiar goal. There is little or no awareness of events outside of what is expected toward goal achievement. So habits support System 1 and blind us toward identifying abnormalities (also known as outliers, or things you would not expect to see in a situation). He says that with a limited ability to recognize and monitor our own shortcomings, our best course is to engage other resources as we attempt to increase these skills you are trying to develop in a specific area.

SPEED DESCRIPTOR 1: QUICKLY DEVELOPS SOLUTIONS

How should "quickly" be defined? Can it be defined as progress that is made evolutionarily, or must it be transformational? There is nothing wrong with improving incrementally. Let us say you wanted to take an incremental approach. Once you determined a baseline for a particular goal or task, you would set a goal that is lower or higher than that baseline. You could make incremental progress by using the behaviors from the *Experimenting, Information Gathering, Collaborating,* and *Feedback Seeking* dimensions. *Interpersonal Risk Taking* might lead you to ask others for help in reaching your goal. *Reflecting* would be useful in reviewing previous attempts before attempting a new trial. After the trial is over, you could measure your results and determine if they were achieved more quickly than during your previous attempt. You can keep trying to improve your performance and stay engaged as long as your speed improves.

The other option is to use a transformational approach to improve speed. Years ago, during the continuous improvement days, I was a participant in a training session. We were tasked with making a product according to specifications and within a set production period. Our team set up a production line with each person assigned a specific responsibility. It was serial in the sense that the second person in the process could not complete their work until the first person finished their task. We ran several timed production trials and improved our time in each trial, starting at about 90 seconds and lowering our time to about 60 seconds. Then the instructor indicated we were to produce not collectively, in our production line, but individually. We each produced products that met the specifications in about 25 or 30 seconds. I was speechless. The change was so obvious, and yet none of us had thought of it.

This is an example of a paradigm shift—looking at a situation in a totally different way. This is part of the *Flexibility* dimension. The behaviors in that dimension are the following:

1. Proposes innovative solutions
2. Considers options before acting
3. Switches among different tasks/jobs
4. Finds common themes
5. Articulates competing ideas/perspectives

None of these behaviors is a direct step to a paradigm shift. Each is a different way to look at a problem or situation to get to that "aha moment." Many entry-level psychology course textbooks, as an example of a paradigm shift, show a picture of a woman. Students are asked to look at the picture and describe what they see. Most people say an old woman. Inevitably, someone will say, "I see a young woman." People cannot see the young woman in the image—until they do. This is the paradigm shift. It uses a change in perception to turn a problem or situation on its head to create a new and different paradigm, or organizing principle.

During the COVID-19 pandemic, I read a blog article in which a group of CEOs shared the lessons they learned during the crisis. The pandemic forced their organizations to go from brick-and-mortar to 97% virtual operations within 24 hours. They indicated that previously, even considering a change of that magnitude would have required a task force and 18 months of meetings and would likely have been deemed too risky to pursue. Then boom—pandemic—and a transformation accomplished "successfully" in 24 hours.

Both approaches are ways to develop solutions more quickly. The first way, incrementally, involves hard work and perseverance. The second approach, transformationally, or paradigm shift, involves Kahneman's approach of moving slowly to go fast. It may take what seems like a longer time to achieve that insight, that flash of brilliance. But once a situation is seen a new way, the progress can be exponential.

SPEED DESCRIPTOR 2: GETS UP TO SPEED ON NEW TASKS/PROJECTS

To illustrate this behavior, you are going to assume the role of a coach. Your goal is to minimize the time required for an employee to reach 100% effectiveness on a project that they know nothing about. Often, the first recommendation for such a situation is total immersion. Since this project is new, if it is the employee's one-and-only priority, and what they live and breathe all day and every day, then immersion should lead the employee to become 100% effective in the shortest amount of time.

That seems plausible if the employee is operating in a vacuum. However, there are two things that you must consider before diving into an immersion activity: What skills and abilities are necessary to do this task/project extremely well, and how well does the person already demonstrate these skills and abilities?

Once you assess this person against a list of knowledge, skills, and abilities (KSAs), you can confirm the components of their development plan, which will need to be integrated with the immersion plan. For example, providing the employee with a particular training experience before exposing them to the immersion activity could accelerate how quickly they absorb the content and learn the new skills. Another approach to try to accelerate learning could be to provide them with relevant information and explain your expectations before immersion.

Other Burke learning agility dimensions that could be introduced at this point to your employee are *Performance Risk Taking, Interpersonal Risk Taking, Information Gathering, Feedback Seeking, Collaborating,* and *Reflecting*. These dimensions could be used in several ways to help them develop the knowledge required for an immersion activity. You could begin the process by assessing their knowledge and skills to identify any gaps. *Collaborating* could be used to *leverage the skills, knowledge, and talents of others*, both within and outside the organization, to develop knowledge. *Information Gathering* could include reading pertinent books and journals on the topic and identifying relevant training programs, webinars, or podcasts. This would be phase 1.

In phase 2, your employee would learn anything that is required to be successful. In the context of speeding up the immersion process, the *Performance Risk Taking* dimension could help. If the plan says it will take them a week to learn the task (100% effectiveness on a new project), how could you condense the time frame to 2 or 3 days? It would likely require *Performance Risk Taking*. For example, they may rate the degree of risk in doing the work in only 3 days as a 6 on a scale of 1 to 7, meaning very risky. An expert might rate the risk as a 4, meaning challenging but possible. The expert would need to show your employee how and why the task is less risky than they think. The employee also could use the *Feedback Seeking* dimension to ask you, their peers, and others about the employee's performance going into the activity and whether they think the accelerated plan is realistic, too hard, or too easy. Using the *Interpersonal Risk-Taking* dimension, the person could request help along with candid opinions on their performance. *Accuracy* is as important here as *Speed* alone. To ensure System 1 and habits are not blinding the employee to abnormalities, you need to put some monitoring mechanism in place so that they know that accuracy is not being sacrificed. Finally, as the person progresses through learning the new task/project, the *Reflecting* dimension can help define things that went well or need to be improved. In an immersion activity, *Reflecting* needs to be a daily and weekly practice. Getting up to speed on new tasks or projects is not a race. It is about moving in the direction of a 7—something you do very well, always.

SPEED DESCRIPTOR 3: READILY GRASPS NEW IDEAS/CONCEPTS

There are similarities between this item and the previous one, *gets up to speed on new tasks/projects*. In this behavior, the individual is *grasping* new ideas and concepts.

Again, suppose you are in the role of a coach. The Burke assessment report would be a starting point in assessing your employee's ability to grasp new ideas or concepts. Answering these questions would also help: Does the employee have a general methodology that they use to learn about a new idea or concept? Can they articulate what they do first, second, etc.? If not, this is where they need to start. The employee could draw on the dimension of *Collaborating* by leveraging the skills, knowledge, and talents of others, which means finding experts in this new area.

Before contacting experts, establish a boundary regarding exactly what the employee is trying to learn to avoid wasting time and effort on things outside of that boundary. If the person does not have an established process for grasping new ideas, they can rely on experts or *Information Gathering* to create one.

At this point, the employee can ask themself these questions to improve in the area of readily grasping new ideas or concepts: Is this idea or concept like another area I previously studied? Is there anything from that study that can be utilized here? How is this idea or concept different or unique? Who are the experts in this area? Are the experts in agreement on this subject or are there different points of view? How will I know if I am not succumbing to habit or System 1's need for *Speed*?

Next, since you are thinking about *Speed*, let us look at which learning agility dimensions can be applied to the descriptor *readily grasps new ideas/concepts*. Your employee could begin by writing down what they are learning. They can contact experts and ask for feedback on their conclusions and use the *Collaborating* dimension to leverage other's expertise. Using *Interpersonal Risk Taking*, the person can challenge, confirm, and clarify what they are learning by consulting with experts. *Performance Risk Taking* provides an opportunity to push out of the comfort zone.

Another idea for getting up to speed quickly in a new area is to teach the content to others. When I am certifying someone to present Burke Learning Agility assessment results, I present the content to the person, then I ask them to present it to me. The gap in understanding often appears in their inability to connect two concepts as they are presenting them. That awareness appears as a moment of terror followed by a blank stare or stammering as the person realizes they do not understand the connection. The moment of embarrassment passes, but the person learns and will never forget the connection going forward.

SPEED DESCRIPTOR 4: ACQUIRES NEW SKILLS AND KNOWLEDGE RAPIDLY

The previous behavior was about grasping new ideas or concepts. This one is about a deep understanding of content. The competency acquisition process, which was described in our first book on learning agility, is a way to measure progress in acquiring a new skill. The five steps in the process are recognition, understanding, self-assessment, skill practice, and practice on the job.

Suppose you are trying to learn how to putt a golf ball. In the recognition step, you watch an in-depth video tutorial about putting: how different greens have different speeds, how to "read" a green, and why you should swing the putter in a pendulum movement.

In the understanding step, you watch a second video of someone putting. You must describe what is being demonstrated in the video and correctly identify the steps. You must be able to describe, for example, that it will be a downhill putt and the putt will break 2 feet from left to right.

In the self-assessment step, you demonstrate the skill, which might include making five putts from different locations on the green, and then rate your skill level. Some call this rating a baseline or starting point. In the Burke Learning Agility Inventory, it appears in the assessment report.

Now that you know your baseline, you practice the skill. In this step, you receive immediate feedback, so you know quickly if you are improving. The skill practice should start in a low-stress environment, so your putting practice should begin on the putting green and eventually move to the course. You need a self-monitoring system so that you can identify performance outside the expected level. You need to stay at step 4 (skill practice) until you "lock in" the desired behavior, or desired number of putts per hole.

In step 5, you demonstrate the skill on the job. In our golf example, it would mean playing an 18-hole round of golf, perhaps in a tournament. As you move to step 5 (practice on the job or, in this case, the course) and the pressure of the situation increases, you may tend to fall back into old bad habits such as swinging the putter with your hands and wrists versus your arms or failing to walk behind a hole to read the greens contours in more than one direction. Thus, the combined importance of *Speed* and *Accuracy*.

Learning quickly could be a sixth step in this skill acquisition process. Here is an illustration of this step that made a big impression on me. Years ago, I worked with Tim Gallwey, the author of *The Inner Game of Tennis*. I saw Tim teach someone who had never before picked up a tennis racket to play intermediate-level tennis in 30 minutes. Mind blowing.

The premise in Gallwey's book is that we all have two voices in our head: Self 1 and Self 2. Self 1 is our natural ability; Self 2 is our inner critic. How do we engage Self 1 to do the things we are capable of and keep Self 2 from interfering? Tim used various techniques to engage the person and take their mind (Self 2) off what Self 1 was doing extremely well. This method aligns well with Daniel Kahneman's System 1 and System 2, which were presented at the beginning of this chapter. According to Kahneman, System 1 gives you quick answers; System 2 slows things down but increases accuracy. With *Speed*, the question often becomes, "How do we introduce the element of faster without negatively affecting the outcome or product?" In truth, it may be better to make incremental changes in some situations. Transformational change will take longer to structure, so allow time for *Reflecting*; it may require *Flexibility* to rethink the framework.

SPEED DESCRIPTOR 5: REACTS WELL TO UNEXPECTED PROBLEMS

The first four behaviors under *Speed* involve doing something faster. This behavior involves quickness in the face of an unplanned obstacle and how well an individual plans for and reacts to it. There are all kinds of examples of this behavior, particularly in sports. Greg Norman's collapse on the back nine of the final day at the 1996 U.S. Masters comes to mind. Helping athletes prepare to perform under pressure is the work of sports psychologists. They help people visualize themselves in various situations and rehearse their responses, so when those or similar situations happen in real life, they execute what they rehearsed.

Athlete or not, most of us can perform effectively under low-stress conditions. Even if the pressure is increased, we can respond appropriately if we have performed the required task many times previously and we acknowledge we feel stressed. Added stress, at least for short periods, can enable some people to perform even better than normal. Institutionalizing a routine that will guard against slipping back into old habits, particularly under pressure, will allow us to reach the desired goal expeditiously.

This relationship between pressure and performance was studied over a century ago by psychologists Robert Yerkes and John Dillingham Dodson and is known as the Yerkes-Dodson law. Yerkes and Dodson determined that increased arousal can help improve performance, but only up to a certain point. At the point when arousal becomes excessive, performance diminishes. For most of us, the challenge become finding just that point but not going beyond it.

As a consultant, I work with leaders in organizations who receive assessment data about themselves from others. Many times, those data do not reflect how the leaders see themselves. In other cases, a leader may realize that during a contentious phone call or meeting they acted in a way that was out of character for them. We talk about techniques they can use to buy them time to give the response they would like to give in stressful situations. We talk about the idea of "clutching." Clutching requires a person to listen to what someone else is saying and not react; instead, pause, take a breath, and reply to the person by saying, "I understand you are upset. Can I get back to you in an hour (or a day or some other point in time)?" That response gives the person under stress the time they need to react effectively to an unexpected problem.

Most of us recognize the exhilaration that comes with doing something quickly and well. The challenge is that moving quickly leaves little room for error. Returning to Kahneman's System 1 and System 2, it is System 2, the voice that slows us down, that may help us most when the unexpected occurs. System 2 engages us to methodically addresses the problem at hand logically and rationally. When the unexpected arises, we may need to sacrifice some output for accuracy. A short-term decrease in productivity is better than a long-term hit to our reputation or the quality of our work product.

A FEW FINAL THOUGHTS ON *SPEED*

Speed is defined as "Acting on ideas quickly so that those that aren't working are discarded and other possibilities are accelerated." In this chapter, *Speed* was broken down into five subcapabilities, which are the items on the Burke assessment. It is these capabilities that give us much deeper insight into what this dimension involves, as speed is not only about the rate at which someone is doing something; it is just as much about knowing when something is not working and adjusting the approach quickly. Or, as Kahneman explains, most of us "don't know what we don't know." We are quicker to recognize when someone else is "off" than to recognize our own failings.

CHAPTER 8

EXPERIMENTING

The Burke definition of Experimenting *is
"Trying out new behaviors (approaches, ideas) to determine what is effective."*

In group sessions on learning agility, I am often asked about the difference between *Experimenting* and *Performance Risk Taking*. *Performance Risk Taking* is "Seeking out new activities (tasks, assignments, roles) that provide an opportunity to be challenged." While it does have similarities to *Experimenting*, the key difference is that *Performance Risk Taking* is more spontaneous. It is more about the challenge and seeing what happens when you are thrust into a situation. *Experimenting* is intentional and programmatic. There are X number of approaches you are going to attempt, and each trial has a purpose. After each trial, *Reflecting* will help you understand what you learned and how those lessons will be used to inform the next trial.

Burke's research identified four sets of behaviors demonstrated by people who were better at *Experimenting*. They are the following:

1. Evaluates new ways of solving problems
2. Experiments with unproven ideas
3. Tries different approaches
4. Learns by trial and error

EXPERIMENTING DESCRIPTOR 1: EVALUATES NEW WAYS OF SOLVING PROBLEMS

Evaluating "new" ways of solving problems implies familiarity with what has been tried before. Let us say you are looking to build your learning agility in this descriptor. Before *Experimenting*, you might use the *Collaborating* behavior of *leverage skills, knowledge, and talents of others*. You could also turn to the behavior of *Information Gathering* by attending a seminar, listening to a podcast, or reading a journal article on the subject. Data collection is *Information Gathering*. Another starting point could be looking at your Burke Learning Agility rating on this behavior; the most proficient Burke assessment rating is a 7, or "always," meaning that evaluating new ways of solving problems is something that is always done and is done extremely well.

Improving this behavior will require monitoring and hard work. The initial step should be to capture all the work you have done in this area of interest and to identify any issues that might be the focus of your future efforts. The employee/learner is trying to improve their current performance in an area and needs to start by looking at all the ways they approached this situation previously. The person uses this approach to collect information or data on themselves to determine what area you are going to work on.

You need to accept that you will not be able to pursue all the issues you identify. Instead, you will need to screen out options by applying criteria such as feasibility (can this new approach even be done?), affordability (what will this experiment cost and is the cost too much?), and time constraints (how long is it going to take to complete the work?). You could use "Yes/No" criteria or a scale ranging from 1 (very easy) to 7 (extremely difficult) to prioritize the options.

After identifying the new aspects of the problem that will be the focus of your experiments you are going to conduct to improve your performance, there will be questions to answer: How many trials will you run? What is the expected outcome of each trial? How will early trials inform and potentially change later experiments? Before ever collecting data, you should identify an expert who is willing to give feedback on the experimental design. This first experimenting behavior is more about planning than doing. The next three behaviors assume this first behavior has been done and are primarily about execution.

EXPERIMENTING DESCRIPTOR 2: EXPERIMENTS WITH UNPROVEN IDEAS

The first behavior in this dimension defines what has been done previously and the options for further experimentation that are feasible from a difficulty, time, and affordability perspective. In this second behavior the focus is on unproven ideas.

This is a chance to use the *Flexibility* behavior of *finds common themes* as you execute experimenting with unproven ideas. This could include asking someone to analyze examples of their work in their area of expertise and identify when they do, and do not, experiment with unproven ideas.

Here is an example. Let us say you're an engineer who does not regularly experiment in unproven ideas when working on projects with people across different cultures such as across business units in your company or internationally for global organizations. You could choose a project that required experimenting with an unproven idea, specifically, an idea that is a 5 or 6 on a difficulty scale where 7 is the most difficult. After conducting the experiments, you would reflect not only on whether your idea was proven true, but what you could do differently to improve the results on a subsequent trial, and whether you learned anything that could be used in a subsequent experiment involving people of different cultures.

Next, you could choose an aspect of the unproven idea (problem) that involves working with people from other cultures with a degree of 2 or 3 on our 7-point scale. Using a couple of the *Collaborating* behaviors, you could ask others if there are changes that should be made to make the project successful in another culture. You should also use *Reflecting* behaviors to review the domestic project: What went well? What was learned? Were there things that went well that might translate or transfer over in a less challenging but also less familiar area? *Flexibility* also plays a role in *switching among different tasks/jobs*. Questions you should ask include: Does the framework used in the project help explain the relationship of variables in this different culture? If not, will using a new framework work better in this different culture?

Switching back and forth between more challenging experiments in more familiar areas and less challenging experiments in less familiar areas can be helpful in reaching the ultimate goal—high challenge in less familiar areas. Over time, the familiarity should increase as well.

EXPERIMENTING DESCRIPTOR 3: TRIES DIFFERENT APPROACHES

Approach is the third aspect we will focus on in the *Experimenting* dimension. It is not our intent to make readers experts in experimental design, but we do need to introduce a few concepts.

The first step in determining approach is to define the research question that needs to be answered and to determine the independent and dependent variables involved. The independent variable is the condition that changes in an experiment; it is the one that can be controlled. It is called an independent variable because it is not affected by any other variable in the experiment. The dependent variable is the one that is affected by a change in the independent variable.

Let us look at two examples, one from sales and another from manufacturing. In the first example, a company is trying to determine the effect of discounting on marketing. The independent variable is the percentage amount of a discount. The dependent variable is sales.

The manufacturing research question is, "What is the ideal length of a work shift?" The dependent variable is number of hours worked. The independent variable is the number of widgets produced. Does the number of hours a person works affect what they produce in that period? Does production go up, go down, or stay constant over time?

Writing out these two choices in a sentence showing cause and effect can help illustrate the difference between independent and dependent variables. If they are in the wrong order, the sentences will not make sense (Helmenstine, 2020).

Let us shift the focus to talent management with the next two examples.

1. The question attempting to be answered: Does the degree of challenge a person experiences affect their rate of development?
    a. Independent variable: Degree of challenge
    b. Dependent variable: Rate of development

Now let us use them in two sentences: "The degree of challenge in an assignment affects the rate of a person's development" makes sense. "The rate of development does not affect the degree of challenge in an assignment" does not make sense.

2. The question attempting to be answered: Does the quantity of feedback a person receives affect their performance?
    a. Independent variable: Quantity of feedback
    b. Dependent variable: Performance

Here are these ideas used in a sentence: "The quantity of feedback affects performance," and "Performance does not affect the quantity of feedback." The first sentence is obviously correct, while the second sounds like nonsense.

Becoming more skillful in *Experimenting* requires using precise terms in the questions that are being answered, being somewhat scientific in setting the variables, and employing basic experimental design principles. For example, using your Burke assessment report as a starting point, you could complete several experiments that require you to vary your approach, reflect, and assess whether you have made progress in improving your skill level. This should include using the *Feedback Seeking* dimension to ask your peers for feedback on your performance. The employee working on the Feedback dimension should ask for feedback in all four behaviors in the *Collaborating* dimension to improve the different ways and people you use to improve your *Experimenting* capability.

EXPERIMENTING DESCRIPTOR 4: LEARNS BY TRIAL AND ERROR

Trial and error is a methodology created by Edward Lee Thorndike in the late 1800s. The approach involves creating a research question, conducting a series of trials or experiments, writing down the results of each, and modifying the trials as necessary, based on the results of previous experiments.

In the preceding "approach" section of this chapter, I used the example of the relationship between discounting a product and resulting sales. Let us say that you are going to conduct five trials on the effect of discounting. Each trial will raise the discount 5%, so trial 1 = 5%, trial 2 = 10%, trial 3 = 15%, trial 4 = 20%, and trial 5 = 25%. Let us assume in the first three trials that sales increase by 5%, 10%, and then only 12% at the 15% discount. In trial 4, rather than go to a 20% discount you decide to increase the discount percent to 17% rather than stay with the original 20% discount. You may have found the discount "ceiling" somewhere above 15%, and it makes more sense to increase the discount at smaller intervals to determine the ultimate ceiling more quickly.

Like the other behavioral approaches to *Experimenting*, the Burke Learning Agility report can be used to identify a baseline skill level. You can use the trial-and-error method to determine if an individual's capability is increasing and attempt to pinpoint the reason why. Using the dimensions of *Collaborating*, *Feedback Seeking*, and *Reflecting* can support improvement efforts.

A FEW MORE THOUGHTS ON *EXPERIMENTING*

Experimenting as a dimension describes actions that are very planful: the learner does a lot of thinking and planning before taking action; the actions are scripted and methodical; the results of one trial could influence subsequent actions. There is a lot of attention paid to observing and recording what occurs. After running some trials, a learner may cycle back to behavior one, "Evaluate new ways of solving problems." Or the learner may shift their attention to the *Reflecting* dimension of learning agility and contemplate how to be more effective in subsequent trials, think about reasons or consequences of the trials conducted, or evaluate the trials to better understand "what happened." When the nine dimensions are initially presented, there is often confusion about the difference between *Experimenting* and *Performance Risk Taking*. In *Experimenting*, there is a lot of thinking and planning. In the next chapter, which is about *Performance Risk Taking*, you will see that it requires seeking new roles and assignments to create personal challenges. In many cases, the assignment involves new territory and there is no plan other than to jump right in.

CHAPTER 9

PERFORMANCE AND INTERPERSONAL RISK TAKING

> *The Burke definition of* Performance Risk Taking *is "Seeking new activities (tasks, assignments, roles) that provide opportunities to be challenged." The Burke definition of* Interpersonal Risk Taking *is "Discussing differences with others in ways that lead to learning and change."*

The concept of risk is something that needs to be understood if it is to be developed. *Performance Risk Taking* is something you do both alone and with others. *Interpersonal Risk Taking* involves interacting with someone else. Clearly, there can be overlap, but initially you should think of them as separate.

As a consultant, I frequently hear "I'm not a risk taker" when I speak with people who are working on improving this learning agility dimension. That leads me to ask them to share specific examples of risk taking and to gauge the level of risk involved, using a rating scale of 1 to 7, with a rating of 1 being low risk and a 7 being high risk. Usually, there is a point in the conversation where two things happen: People quantify risk taking, and they realize that each person's quantification of risk is different. It usually becomes clear that a situation that one person might rate a 2 could in fact be a 4 for someone else. This does not mean that one person's rating is right and the other is wrong, or that one is better or worse. It just means that everyone's idea of risk taking is unique to them.

So why is being able to gauge the level of risk fundamental to developing someone's ability in the area of *Performance Risk Taking*? If you are a learner working with a coach, you need a common language with which to communicate. You both need to reach an agreement on the level of risk (from 1 to 7) that exists in a situation. A shared understanding of the risk level of a situation allows you and your coach to explore the aspects of the situation to be able to affect the risk level. Two people may use a different scale to evaluate the same situation. Until a common scale is used by both people, they cannot be compared. Both people need to be aligned and use the same scale in order to work on increasing or decreasing the risk-level situation. Once a common scale is used the two people may determine that they have different interpretations of how risky the same situation is.

Research regarding goal setting shows us that people perform best in situations that are both *realistic* (able to be accomplished) and *challenging* (not too easy or too hard). Finding that middle ground where something is both realistic and challenging can be difficult. Using the risk-taking scale example, goals that are too realistic would be rated in the 1 to 2 range, and those that are too challenging would be rated in the 6 to 7 range. People perform best in the 3 to 5 area, where the goals are neither too easy nor too hard.

Time and resources are additional factors that may contribute to the level of risk in a situation.

For example:

- *Time:* This involves how much time you have to complete a task. If you shorten or lengthen the time frame of a task, it can affect the level of risk involved.
- *Resources:* This can involve either physical or financial resources. For example, if you are given a project and need to complete the work personally, instead of being given a team to assist you, this would certainly affect the level of risk you would assign to the project. Financial resources, equipment, or expertise can also impact the level of risk in a situation.

In my previous career, the U.S.-based organization I worked for was acquired by a South African company. The U.S. company also had offices in Munich, Germany. I was given the challenging assignment of closing down the German operation. Additionally, I was told not to return until the task was completed with no lawsuits against the organization. I was the only internal resource on the project and negotiated a substantial budget to accomplish the task. I also engaged a local consultant with expertise in German labor law.

The German consultant and I met with each employee and attempted to negotiate a signed release in exchange for a severance package. The first round of meetings successfully resolved any issues with about 75% of the employees. Each signed the release and took the severance package offered. We then scheduled meetings with the remaining employees. In about 20% of these cases, the employees had personal concerns that needed to be addressed and resolved before they would sign the release. The remaining 5% of the employees required more effort before they signed a release. We continued to negotiate and address their issues until they accepted the terms of the severance package. I returned to the United States; mission accomplished.

Time and resources are often needed to reduce performance risk. However, in this case, I didn't have these options. I felt that if I did not accept the assignment, I would most likely be terminated. If any lawsuits were filed, I also would likely be terminated. My task of getting resignations from all the German employees was a crummy assignment and something I had never done before, or since, thankfully. I had to become knowledgeable in German labor laws very quickly, and I had to create a process whereby we met and dealt with every employee.

At this point, I am going to switch focus to behaviorally define *Performance Risk Taking*. Warner Burke's research that collectively constituted learning agility identified nine different capabilities. He defined the *Performance Risk Taking* capability as "seeking new activities (tasks, assignments, roles) that provide opportunities to be challenged." The four ways this dimension was demonstrated are the following:

1. **Takes on challenging roles**
2. **Engages in ambiguous tasks**
3. **Embraces work that is risky**
4. **Volunteers for projects that involve the possibility of failure**

Back to the example of closing the Munich operations for my former company. I considered the assignment to be rated in the 6+ range of risk taking. The instructions I was given were clear: Return with no lawsuits against the organization and obtain releases from all employees. How I was to get that done was very ambiguous. On one level, I did volunteer for the assignment, but on another level, I truly saw no alternative that would keep me employed. I successfully completed the assignment of closing the German office and returned to the United States, only to find that the remainder of the international operations of my former company had been integrated into the acquiring company's European operation. My old job no longer existed. "Fortunately," I was then appointed Vice President of Human Resources for North America of the acquiring company, with the mission of integrating the HR systems of the six legacy companies (all acquisitions). Two people had previously attempted this assignment and failed. Clearly, this was another assignment with a 6–7 level of performance risk. In the rest of this chapter, I will discuss *Performance Risk Taking* and how to help individuals develop the capabilities and behaviors that describe this dimension.

PERFORMANCE RISK FRAMEWORK

Below is a potential framework you can use to assess the performance risk of an assignment and then raise or lower the risk as appropriate. It may also assist learners and their coaches with what aspects of an assignment they need to focus on to maximize the assignment's manageability. The risk framework takes each of the items under the *Performance Risk Taking* dimension and turns them into a scale that can be used to evaluate risk.

The scales in this section can be used to quantify risk taking. Each scale has a minimum value of 1 and a maximum value of 7. There are four factors of *Performance Risk Taking*; therefore, the value for each description must be added together to quantify the overall *Performance Risk Taking* value for an assignment. The lowest total *Performance Risk Taking* value of an assignment would therefore be 4 and the highest value would be 28. As discussed earlier, a moderate risk assignment (realistic and challenging) would be in the 12 to 23 range.

TAKES ON CHALLENGING ROLES

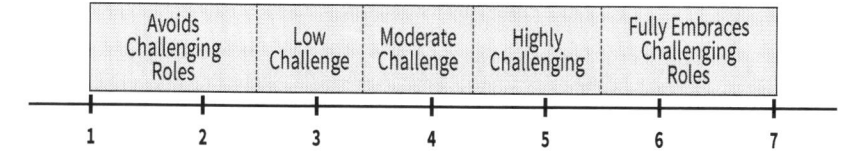

Avoids Challenging Roles	Low Challenge	Moderate Challenge	Highly Challenging	Fully Embraces Challenging Roles
1 2	3	4	5	6 7

ENGAGES IN AMBIGUOUS TASKS

Does Not Embrace	Detached	Moderately Embraces	Embraces	Fully Embraces
1 2	3	4 5	6	7

EMBRACES WORK THAT IS RISKY

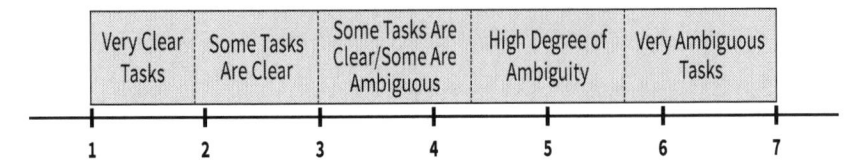

Very Clear Tasks	Some Tasks Are Clear	Some Tasks Are Clear/Some Are Ambiguous	High Degree of Ambiguity	Very Ambiguous Tasks
1 2	3	4 5	6	7

VOLUNTEERS FOR PROJECTS THAT INVOLVE THE POSSIBILITY OF FAILURE

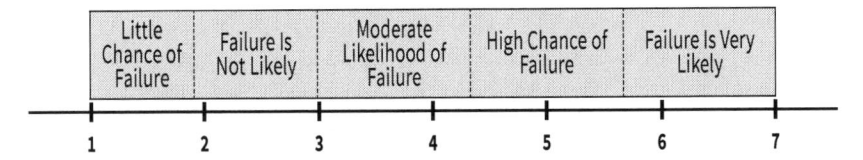

Little Chance of Failure	Failure Is Not Likely	Moderate Likelihood of Failure	High Chance of Failure	Failure Is Very Likely
1 2	3	4 5	6	7

When attempting to determine the performance risk level of an assignment, the performance risk factors above may be added, or the overall framework below may be used.

OVERALL PERFORMANCE RISK

Low Performance Risk	0–11 Points
Moderate Performance Risk	12–23 Points
High Performance Risk	24–28 Points

Once a job or assignment is assessed to determine the level of performance risk, the factors could be increased or decreased by adding or removing resources to either increase or decrease the risk level. For example, using the factor of *engages in ambiguous tasks*, a supervisor could increase the risk level by providing less information to the learner. By doing so, the supervisor is engaging the learner to be more proactive in obtaining the information needed to succeed. If the reverse is true and the assignment is determined to be overly ambiguous, the supervisor could attempt to increase the learner's clarity or provide a second person with previous experience in the area to use as a resource.

Let's look at a specific assignment across all four factors in the performance risk area and determine how to lower the overall level of risk across the factors. In this example, the learner is chosen for an international assignment, which is traditionally considered a way to test and challenge someone and thereby potentially develop their learning agility. A typical international assignment lasts for 3 years; this assignment will require the learner to relocate to the assigned country with their family. International assignments are very expensive for an organization, costing approximately $1 million over a 3-year period. An organization may be more willing to make this investment if the learner has the critical technical expertise needed in the location and is seen as having the potential to make a greater contribution to the organization in the future. Next is a risk level rating of the international assignment for each of the four factors.

INTERNATIONAL ASSIGNMENT EXAMPLE

Takes on challenging roles. The reason this aspect of an international assignment is rated high risk is that in addition to doing work in a function like finance or human resources, you have to do the job in a situation where you likely don't know the local language or culture. Your family that accompanies you has to deal with those same issues of language and culture. These were not concerns for family members in the home location. People who have been on international assignments report it takes about 50% more time to complete the same amount work you would do in your home country.

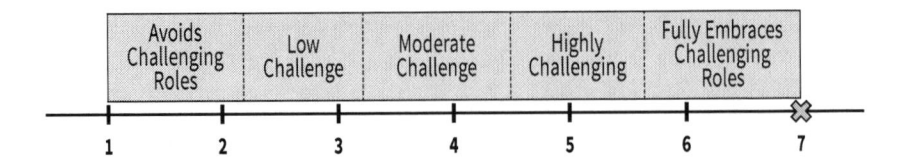

Avoids Challenging Roles	Low Challenge	Moderate Challenge	Highly Challenging	Fully Embraces Challenging Roles
1	2	3	4	5	6	7

Embraces work that is risky. This category is rated a "7" because being successful in this new country means you need to be flexible enough to learn how things are done locally. You need to learn how to communicate with others in a potentially different way.

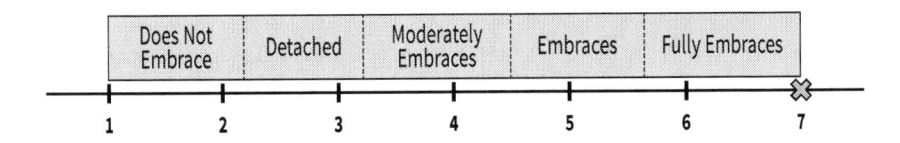

Does Not Embrace	Detached	Moderately Embraces	Embraces	Fully Embraces
1	2	3	4	5	6	7

Engages in ambiguous tasks. The degree of ambiguity is rated a "7" because there is a lot of confusion in communications requiring using two different languages to discuss an issue. The way something is done in the assignee's home country may be 100% different in this foreign location. The resources the assignee had in the home country are likely not available or wouldn't be helpful in this different environment.

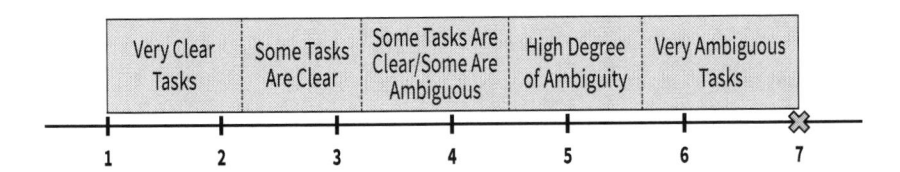

Very Clear Tasks	Some Tasks Are Clear	Some Tasks Are Clear/Some Are Ambiguous	High Degree of Ambiguity	Very Ambiguous Tasks
1	2	3	4	5	6	7

Volunteers for projects that involve the possibility of failure. The reason that failure is high is that there are so many aspects of the job that are different than you knew how to do in your home country. Figuring out "how" things work and doing the work in a timely fashion is harder to do, and thus you need to work longer hours. Your family is dealing with the same pressures of language and culture. They would like to turn to you, but you are working. There are all kinds of reasons that an assignment fails. There are numerous examples of couple divorcing, a child getting into trouble and needing to go home, or substance abuse issues as the family unit is looking for ways to cope.

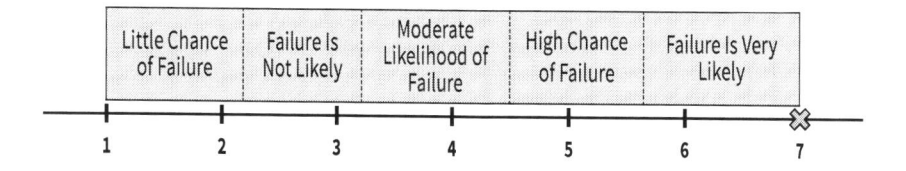

Little Chance of Failure	Failure Is Not Likely	Moderate Likelihood of Failure	High Chance of Failure	Failure Is Very Likely
1	2	3	4	5	6	7

According to this rating, the overall performance risk level of this international assignment is in the "high" range of 24 to 28 points. The only area that may be open to interpretation is *embraces work that is risky*. This factor was rated high risk because the learner would need to relocate their entire family to the foreign location and to fully embrace the situation to be effective.

To make this international assignment a lower performance risk, the organization could implement several solutions, listed below. Some options could be implemented at a later point if the learner is truly struggling.

REDUCING THE ASSIGNMENT'S CHALLENGES

The following solutions are presented by performance factor.

TAKES ON CHALLENGING ROLES

- Identify the top five areas that define why the assignment is challenging.
- Determine solutions to reduce each of the top five challenges.
- Determine if any family concerns are affecting the learner's performance.

- Determine if there are any local resources that can address the family's concerns.
- Provide cross-cultural training for the family.

ENGAGES IN AMBIGUOUS TASKS
- Clearly define deliverables and due dates.
- Determine accountability for deliverables.
- Provide cross-cultural training to the learner.

EMBRACES WORK THAT IS RISKY
- Find a strong performer with previous international experience who can be added to the learner's team.
- Find a local coach with international and cross-cultural experience in both the home and host countries of the learner.

VOLUNTEERS FOR PROJECTS THAT INVOLVE THE POSSIBILITY OF FAILURE
- Define what failure could look like.
- Identify strategies to prevent failure from occurring.
- Find a mentor in both the home and host countries with whom the learner can discuss any problems or issues as they arise.
- Communicate to the learner who the technical and financial resource people are and how they can be made available.

As the learner moves along in the assignment, it will be important for their coach to use the learning agility dimensions of *Speed*, *Flexibility*, and *Reflecting*. *Speed* and *Flexibility* are the essence of learning agility. *Reflecting* is the part of learning agility where the learner must recognize the value of slowing down and thinking about how to improve their result.

Speed
- Quickly develops solutions
- Gets up to speed on new tasks/projects

- Readily grasps new ideas/concepts
- Acquires new skills and knowledge rapidly
- Reacts well to unexpected problems

Flexibility
- Proposes innovative solutions
- Considers options before acting
- Switches among different tasks/jobs
- Finds common themes
- Articulates competing ideas/perspectives

Reflecting
- Reflects on work processes and projects
- Reflects on how to be more effective
- Considers reasons for and consequences of actions or events
- Evaluates events with others to understand what happened

A FEW FINAL THOUGHTS ON *PERFORMANCE RISK TAKING*

Remember that *Speed* and *Flexibility* are the drivers of learning agility. *Reflecting* is something you should do after every learning agility activity. What should you consider from *Speed* as it relates to *Performance Risk Taking*? The difference between winning and not winning a contract may come down to who can complete something faster; it also involves that balance between speed and accuracy. Finally, what is your strategy for dealing with unexpected problems? While you are figuring out the ambiguous parts of the project, what is your Plan B and Plan C? How are you going to go back to the place where you were certain, before the ambiguity began?

If you are considering aspects of *Flexibility* when you are working through a performance risk, are you finding common themes among the ambiguity? When you are assessing the risk of a situation, can you articulate the competing ideas? How do you look at your challenge in a different way, or change the framework? The inclination of performance risk takers is to jump into the situation; an aspect of *Flexibility* is to consider options before taking action.

Performance risk takers do not necessarily step back from the action of the project and reflect. Instead, they need to consider these questions: Are the processes being used sound, or could they be improved? How? What is not working and how could we refine it to be more effective?

Performance Risk Taking is critical in learning agility situations when *what* to do is unclear and unknown. There are ways to adjust the risk level that have already been described. *Speed*, *Flexibility*, and *Reflecting* can add clarity and will lead to a better solution.

INTERPERSONAL RISK TAKING

Let us shift our attention to another aspect of risk taking: *Interpersonal Risk Taking*. The key issue in *Interpersonal Risk Taking* is self-awareness. From a coach's perspective, self-awareness involves how well learners know their areas of strength and weakness. Can they differentiate between content and process? Are they self-confident? (There is a difference between arrogance and self-confidence.) Are they confident enough to see strength in asking others for help when needed? Are they comfortable enough with themselves to state an opinion not held by others and to pursue that opinion while being opposed by others?

To give you a better sense of what *Interpersonal Risk-Taking* looks like, below is a personal example from my work at Anheuser-Busch. I had taken over the management development function and saw huge opportunities to improve the programs being offered. For example, one of the responsibilities in this role was developing the agenda for and executing a senior management conference. Before my tenure, the conference was entertaining, but I thought it did not provide enough strategic content and ideas for senior-level managers. Attendees of the previous year's conference included 75 individuals from senior leadership roles but few of the organization's key senior leaders. My goal was to create a conference that would be attended by the top 200 leaders of the organization and for the CEO to "open" the event. My measure of success? Having to turn potential attendees away because full enrollment had been reached.

As I began working on this goal, I created a steering committee of 20 key senior leaders in the organization. I met with them individually once they agreed to participate on the committee and asked for their input on topics to be discussed and possible presenters. In some cases, I even attempted to influence their ideas for topics. Eventually, I assembled their input into a proposed agenda and presented it to them as a group.

My proposed agenda showed that the CEO would open the conference. Many members of the steering committee felt that the CEO should have a role in the conference, while others did not think he would agree to participate. Ultimately, the committee endorsed the agenda.

I collaborated with several committee members to use their contacts to confirm presenters. My next goal was to confirm the CEO as the conference opener. Because I was three levels below the CEO in the organization, I worked with the Senior Vice President of Human Resources to request that the CEO participate. After he met with the Senior Vice President, the CEO agreed to open the conference.

The CEO kicked off the conference with nearly 200 senior leaders in attendance. He did an outstanding job and came away from the event recognizing the opportunity it offered to influence his senior managers. The conference helped surface many important organizational issues and identified ways to pursue them after the conference ended. The problem was that, following the CEO's presentation, many attendees left the conference. The next year, I asked the CFO to open the conference and the CEO to close the event, and both agreed. That year, no attendee left the meeting early.

The Burke behavioral definitions of *Interpersonal Risk Taking* are the following:

1. Brings up tough issues with others
2. Asks others for help

3. Discusses mistakes with others
4. Challenges others' ideas even when they are shared by many

Using these factors of *Interpersonal Risk Taking*, how risky was the situation of changing the senior-level conference for me? One tough issue was questioning the worthiness of what had been offered previously. My immediate supervisor had served as the moderator of the previous conference, so changing the conference was, in a way, criticizing his past efforts. That made this effort fairly high-risk for me. I had to ask senior managers to serve on the steering committee and get their input. I had to ask the Senior Vice President of Human Resources to obtain the CEO's agreement to address the first conference I organized. When planning the conference, I had also asked prior participants for their feedback and asked the steering committee for areas that could be improved. I also received unsolicited feedback from my boss, his boss, and the CEO on ways the conference could be improved.

Once the prior conference attendees started challenging organizational norms, I knew we were going in the right direction. When challenged, organizations do not necessarily respond the way you prefer. In this case, the organization resisted. The conference attendees wanted the Executive Team to attend the conference. The Executive Team said no, they had their own meeting. The conference attendees identified several changes they felt needed to be made in order to improve the operations of one of the business units. The conference attendees' suggestion was ignored by the Executive Team. So, senior managers were making positive suggestions coming out of subjects presented at the conference. They expected something positive was going to happen, but the Executive Team put them off.

Knowing when to pursue and when to yield is not always clear in these situations. In the context of *Interpersonal Risk Taking*, it is the idea of an initial challenge in the face of opposition that is important.

I will use the same framework to develop *Interpersonal Risk Taking* as with *Performance Risk Taking*. I will also use the concept of quantifying the risk in a situation so that a coach and the leader that they are working with are viewing the situation in the same way.

The behavioral descriptors will be used to create scales to measure each of the four aspects of *Interpersonal Risk Taking*. Each scale has a minimum value of 1 and a maximum value of 7. There are four aspects of *Interpersonal Risk Taking*, which means that the value for each aspect must be added together to find the total *Interpersonal Risk Taking* value of an assignment. The lowest total *Interpersonal Risk Taking* value of an assignment would be 4 and the highest value would be 28. As discussed earlier, a moderate risk assignment (realistic and challenging) would be in the 12 to 23 range.

Low Interpersonal Risk	0–11 Points
Moderate Interpersonal Risk	12–23 Points
High Interpersonal Risk	24–28 Points

SENIOR MANAGEMENT CONFERENCE EXAMPLE

BRINGS UP TOUGH ISSUES WITH OTHERS

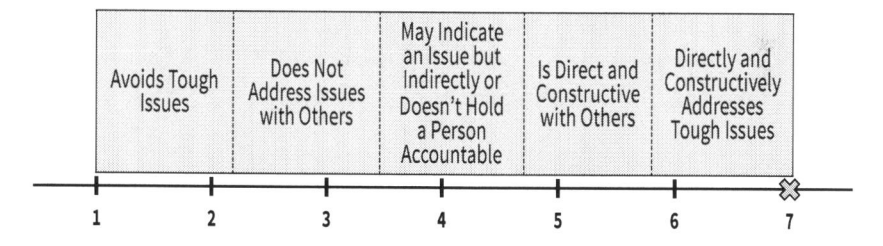

| Avoids Tough Issues | Does Not Address Issues with Others | May Indicate an Issue but Indirectly or Doesn't Hold a Person Accountable | Is Direct and Constructive with Others | Directly and Constructively Addresses Tough Issues |

1   2   3   4   5   6   7

ASKS OTHERS FOR HELP

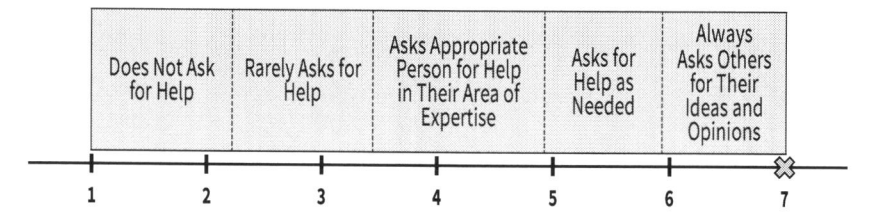

| Does Not Ask for Help | Rarely Asks for Help | Asks Appropriate Person for Help in Their Area of Expertise | Asks for Help as Needed | Always Asks Others for Their Ideas and Opinions |

1   2   3   4   5   6   7

DISCUSSES MISTAKES WITH OTHERS

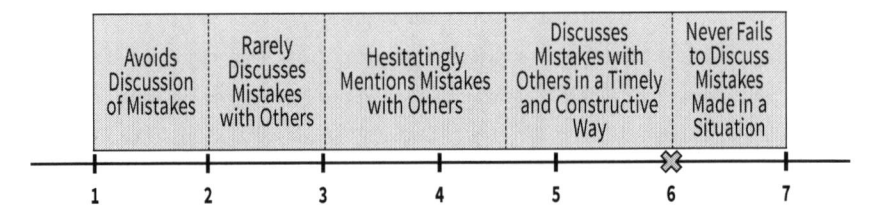

Avoids Discussion of Mistakes	Rarely Discusses Mistakes with Others	Hesitatingly Mentions Mistakes with Others	Discusses Mistakes with Others in a Timely and Constructive Way	Never Fails to Discuss Mistakes Made in a Situation

1   2   3   4   5   6 ✗   7

CHALLENGES OTHERS' IDEAS EVEN WHEN THEY ARE SHARED BY MANY

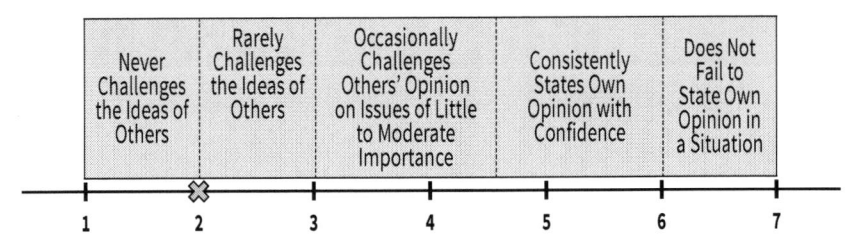

Never Challenges the Ideas of Others	Rarely Challenges the Ideas of Others	Occasionally Challenges Others' Opinion on Issues of Little to Moderate Importance	Consistently States Own Opinion with Confidence	Does Not Fail to State Own Opinion in a Situation

1   2 ✗   3   4   5   6   7

According to this rating, the overall interpersonal risk level of changing the senior management conference is 22, in the moderate range of 12 to 23. Raising or lowering the risk could be accomplished by modifying one or more of the four areas. Consider another example: working on a task force.

EXAMPLE: DISORGANIZED TASK FORCE

Task forces are often employed by organizations to address a problem or an opportunity. They are typically staffed with individuals who have relevant technical expertise. The task force may appoint a facilitator, or the role may be assigned to the most senior member of the group. The overall objective of the group is typically given by a sponsor or the person who identified the problem or opportunity.

In this example, suppose your manager, knowing you are working on *Interpersonal Risk Taking*, asked you to take over as facilitator of a task force. (The task force has been meeting for a while, and you are asked to join and serve as the group's facilitator). The task force has been plagued by a plethora of initial confusion regarding duties, responsibilities, decision making, boundaries, and resources. The group has a deadline but has worked for weeks and made little progress. As the facilitator, you feel unstated pressure from the CEO to see results. How would you diagnose the issues within this task force and go about assisting them?

BRINGS UP TOUGH ISSUES WITH OTHERS

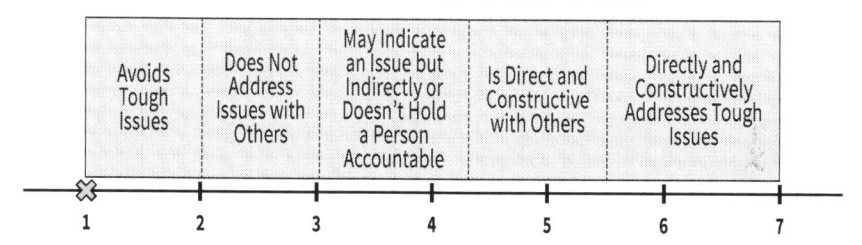

Avoids Tough Issues	Does Not Address Issues with Others	May Indicate an Issue but Indirectly or Doesn't Hold a Person Accountable	Is Direct and Constructive with Others	Directly and Constructively Addresses Tough Issues
1	2	3	4	5	6	7

(marker at 1)

After introducing yourself to the members of the task force, you find there are several problematic issues known by members of the group that have not been made explicit. As an initial step, the issues need to be discussed and understood by all task force members. Prioritizing those issues and determining how to address them are critical to the group's success.

ASKS OTHERS FOR HELP

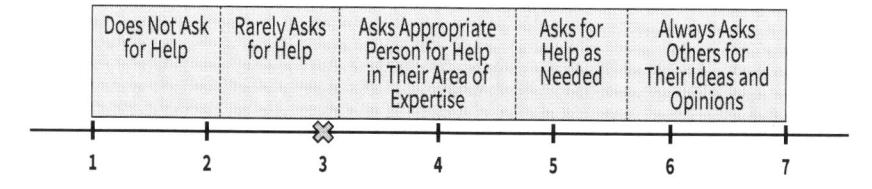

Does Not Ask for Help	Rarely Asks for Help	Asks Appropriate Person for Help in Their Area of Expertise	Asks for Help as Needed	Always Asks Others for Their Ideas and Opinions
1	2	3	4	5	6	7

(marker at 3)

In part, your involvement in the task force is as a source of help. Once the issues above are made explicit, your role as facilitator may make it possible for the group to determine the need for other resources to accomplish their mission. You can help guide the group to see that asking for additional help is appropriate.

DISCUSSES MISTAKES WITH OTHERS

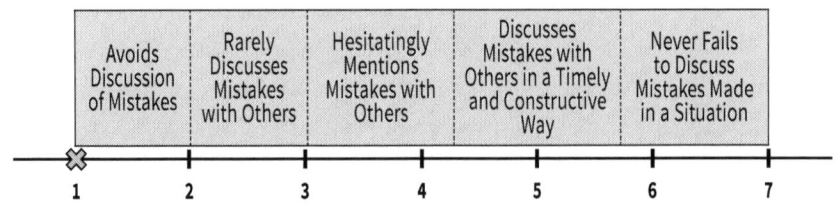

Avoids Discussion of Mistakes	Rarely Discusses Mistakes with Others	Hesitatingly Mentions Mistakes with Others	Discusses Mistakes with Others in a Timely and Constructive Way	Never Fails to Discuss Mistakes Made in a Situation
1	2	3	4	5	6	7

Since "process" components were not discussed when the task force was initially assembled, the person with the strongest personality took over and ran the group without getting input from anyone else in the group. It was clear to many in the group that this approach would not work, but no one verbalized their concerns. After interviewing task force members, you determine that you, as a neutral third party, should clarify and discuss this with the group. With your assistance, the group can decide the direction in which to proceed.

CHALLENGES OTHERS' IDEAS EVEN WHEN THEY ARE SHARED BY MANY

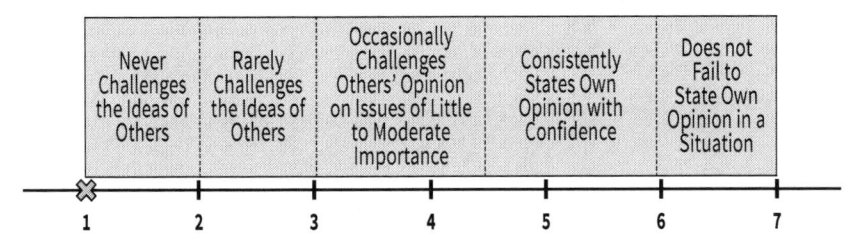

Never Challenges the Ideas of Others	Rarely Challenges the Ideas of Others	Occasionally Challenges Others' Opinion on Issues of Little to Moderate Importance	Consistently States Own Opinion with Confidence	Does not Fail to State Own Opinion in a Situation
1	2	3	4	5	6	7

You have an overall score on this project of 6 out of 28. This indicates that there is a lot of risk against this being successful. There is a good chance that the group will not accomplish its mission. This is then translated into a risk level of high. You will have to identify resources that will allow you to increase the score above the moderate level, or to the 12 to 23 range.

To summarize, the members of the task force are having difficultly functioning effectively. The group members are not expressing their concerns, and one person is taking control of the group and causing others to be silent. These issues are often the most difficult to address in the

Interpersonal Risk Taking dimension. As the external facilitator, whose role is it to be neutral? This person needs to diagnose how the group is functioning. The facilitator needs to elicit the group's support on how often and how deeply they want to address these difficult issues. If the group addresses an uncomfortable issue successfully, it will likely increase their willingness to address other issues.

The process of addressing the *Interpersonal Risk Taking dimension* begins with diagnosing who or what is causing the group to not function effectively. The facilitator can then decide how slowly or quickly they will intervene.

As learners move along in this assignment or one like it, you or the coach should consider using the learning agility factors of *Speed*, *Flexibility*, and *Reflecting* as they pertain to the *Interpersonal Risk Taking dimension* (see below).

SPEED

- Quickly develops solutions
- Gets up to speed on new tasks/project
- Readily grasps new ideas/concepts
- Acquires new skills and knowledge rapidly
- Reacts well to unexpected problems

FLEXIBILITY

- Proposes innovative solutions
- Considers options before acting
- Switches between different tasks/jobs
- Finds common themes
- Articulates competing ideas/perspectives

REFLECTING

- Reflects on work processes and projects
- Reflects on how to be more effective
- Considers reasons for and consequences of actions or events
- Evaluates events with others to understand what happened

A FEW FINAL THOUGHTS ON *INTERPERSONAL RISK TAKING*

Interpersonal Risk Taking is about courage. It is about looking inward at your own shortcomings and getting help to improve. It is speaking up and sharing your point of view with others with the intent of a better result, and speaking up quickly so that corrective action can be taken. Being able to state a contrary perspective may require you to get up to speed on a new topic quickly. Having a contrary point of view may open the door for others to add to or modify that viewpoint.

Flexibility in support of *Interpersonal Risk Taking* might look like presenting an issue in a totally different way. You might look at different aspects of a work problem and determine how it is similar to or different from a previous project. Having the courage to state a different point of view may lead to an outcome that would never have been surfaced. Raising a tough issue may cause a group to consider other options before proceeding. It may be uncomfortable to ask a tough question, but the question may cause your team to step back and look at and refine its processes and realize they could make a modification that would improve the solution. Sometimes there is time pressure on a project; asking a question before taking action could ultimately save time and money. Performing a postmortem on a project may allow your team to learn what they did or could have done that will enable them to be more effective in the future.

Interpersonal Risk Taking is about doing things that will lead to greater self-awareness. This should improve performance over time. Asking difficult questions is not always easy. When done tactfully, however, it can be transformational. The ability to see things differently than everyone else is a gift. Others may not embrace the contrary idea initially; that is why it is called a risk. Over time, if those risks lead to insights and better solutions, you will find that your ideas will receive a fair hearing, even if some think of you as harebrained.

CHAPTER 10

COLLABORATING

The Burke definition of Collaborating *is "Finding ways to work with others that generate unique opportunities for learning."*

As a graduate student at Teachers College, Columbia University in the 1970s, I was fortunate to learn a lesson about *Collaborating* that continues to boggle my mind. Have you heard the phrase "seven degrees of separation," or played the trivia game "Seven Degrees of Kevin Bacon"? If so, this story will interest you.

While at Columbia, I took a class with a professor named Charles Kadushin. He was an expert in network theory, an aspect of *Collaborating*. One day in class, he said that you could locate someone anywhere in the world who you did not know with seven connections. I was intrigued but at the same time found the idea mind-boggling. This was the time before personal computers, smartphones, and social media. Communication tools were handwritten or typewritten letters, landline telephones, and telephone books that listed addresses and home telephone number. I believed what Professor Kadushin said, and contemplated which person I might want to reach, who would be my first connection, who would be my second, and so on.

I got a chance to use this networking/collaborating capability while at Columbia University on a research study called Project Talent. It was a longitudinal, national study of people who had graduated from high school in a certain year. They contacted people every five years to see how their lives and careers were progressing. Most people responded to the follow-up questionnaires. The part of the project that I worked on were the nonrespondents. People had moved; gotten married and changed their last name. My job was to find them and get them to answer the questionnaire with me on the telephone. This was in 1972, no cell phones, no computers. I started making telephone calls to find relatives of the person I wanted to reach. Through a series of calls I found out who their friends had been. I called them and they in turn suggested other people and so on and so on. I was so successful that the researchers kept giving me additional lists of names of their "nonrespondents." I began to learn these capabilities with Professor Kadushin.

About the same time, I was also working as a college administrator overseeing all the noncredit business and management courses at Long Island University. One instructor taught several of the real estate classes in our course offerings. He was 30 years older than me and had a very successful real estate business. I saw him as someone I could learn from. One of the things he told me was that every time you meet someone, get their business card. Put it in a Rolodex (old-school contacts file) or a three-ring binder where you can insert pages to file the business cards. I never forgot his advice. I started collecting business cards, and I still have several books of them. When I started working internationally for Anheuser-Busch in the 1980s, I created separate books for contacts in the United Kingdom, continental Europe, Mexico, Japan, and Asia. All that information helped me tremendously in reaching people I needed to help me accomplish my job. I urge everyone I talk to, no matter their industry or vocation, to collect and use contacts in some form.

Here is an example. Shortly after I moved to Wilmington, North Carolina, in 2013, my company, E.A.S.I-Consult®, started producing a monthly newsletter to market our capabilities to our target audience. The firm that assisted us was the *Wilmington Business Journal*. Their staff started talking to us about using social media, something I had heard about but did not fully understand. I took the time to listen and realized it was not that different from collecting business cards. Today, I have more than 16,000 connections in my LinkedIn network. They represent people from all over the world. Every time I meet someone new, I add them as a connection.

The purpose of these stories is to make a few points about the importance of *Collaborating*. *Collaborating* is something that you must commit to doing and to do over time. During my career, I have worked with people who were between jobs. They understood that networking was instrumental to getting their next position. Many people begin assembling a good network when job searching but let their network atrophy once they get that next position. At some point in the future, however, they may need to transition jobs again, and rue the day that they stopped maintaining and developing the network they had begun.

I do not want you to think that *Collaborating* is the same thing as networking. Networking is only one part of what is required in *Collaborating*. Burke determined four sets of behaviors that defined *Collaborating*, as follows:

1. Leverages skills, knowledge, and talents of others
2. Works with colleagues from different backgrounds
3. Collaborates with other parts of the organization
4. Asks stakeholders for their point of view

We will look at each of these behaviors individually to understand how these capabilities can be developed.

COLLABORATING DESCRIPTOR 1: LEVERAGES SKILLS, KNOWLEDGE, AND TALENTS OF OTHERS

What does that really mean? How do you take what other people know (knowledge) and things that they are good at (skills and talents) and use that to accomplish something? If you had a vast network of contacts, wouldn't you be in a stronger position than someone without that network?

This discussion of *Collaborating* can be expanded to include the learning agility dimension of *Flexibility*. Remember, *Flexibility* is "Being open to new ideas and proposing new solutions." It is reframing a situation to find a different way to describe the relationship of the variables involved.

During the coronavirus pandemic of 2020, there was an acute shortage of ventilators. Historically, the ventilator market has been limited, occupied by a few small companies to manufacture them. During the pandemic, many U.S. manufacturing facilities, including those owned by General Motors, shut down operations to stop the spread of the virus in their facilities. So, you had an idle manufacturing workforce with the ability to assemble a car in 18 hours or less. You also had a technically capable ventilator company, Ventec Life Systems, that had the ability to make ventilators but lacked the knowledge or facility to scale their operations quickly.

On March 20, 2020, GM and Ventec started discussing how they might work together to solve the problem of the ventilator shortage. They reached agreements on roles and responsibilities, globally sourced parts, established a manufacturing process, and produced a quality product in just over a month. On April 27, 2020, the first ventilator produced by their joint efforts came off a line in a repurposed GM manufacturing plant in Kokomo, Indiana. This process required everyone involved to exhibit *Flexibility* in thinking. Six weeks earlier, neither side could have imagined themselves in a relationship with the other, or being open to different ways to approach a production task where one of the partners had no experience.

This is an example of how two organizations were able to *leverage the skills, knowledge, and talent of others*. What does that look like at the individual or team level? In making a development assignment, you could add a person to a task force that was completely out of the person's area of expertise to give them the chance to learn and think differently. You would talk with the person joining the task force about why they are being added and what you want them to learn about *Collaborating*. In a best case scenario, they may contribute something that would not have been suggested by the other members in the group. At the end of their task force experience, you would have another conversation about learning. What did they learn about *Collaborating*? How can they take what they learned about *Collaborating* and use it in the future?

Other examples of leveraging skills would be putting a marketing person on a project with a finance group, or putting a person with international experience on a task force dealing with a domestic issue. In any of these examples, the outsider needs to be empowered. The finance group or the domestic issue task force group needs to know that this person is joining to help expand their thinking or bring new ideas to the group. This is going to require the outsider to use the *Interpersonal Risk Taking* behavior of *brings up tough issues with others*. There will likely be a tendency of the group to dismiss this different point of view. The team will have to devote time to reflecting about what they learned from the newcomer. This process will not always result in a "big" idea. The overall objective is to leverage other people's talents, skills, and knowledge to add value to the team's capabilities.

COLLABORATING DESCRIPTOR 2: WORKS WITH COLLEAGUES FROM DIFFERENT BACKGROUNDS

This is similar to the preceding behavior. In both cases, you are bringing someone with a different perspective into an existing group. In this second behavior, work with colleagues from different backgrounds. The entire group is made up of different or unique individuals. The thing these individuals have in common is that they are all different. Assume the project is solving an engineering problem. In addition to a couple engineers, you might add a person from operations, a person from finance, a person from sales, marketing, and human resources. Except for the engineers, all of the other group members represent other functions and other points of view.

Here is an example. Suppose you are assigned to a task force to solve a problem facing your organization. Each task force member represents a different functional group from the organization; all disciplines are represented and at the table to solve the problem. The task force may be required to demonstrate *Flexibility* by looking at the problem in a totally different way. Each member may need to gather information and to use *Interpersonal Risk Taking* with each other by asking for help and bringing up tough issues.

Several years ago, I attended a 10-day cross-cultural program at a business school in Europe to evaluate the possible use of the program in my company. The participants represented most of the countries in Europe, and I was the only American. The class was divided into several groups and charged with solving a problem. We were to present our solution on the last day of the program. Our group decided to go to dinner after class to discuss our project. We had a great dinner, with good conversation and quite a bit of wine. The project was never discussed. At the end of the evening, the fact that the project had not been addressed was mentioned. We decided that we should go to dinner again the following night, and I suggested that we be more task-oriented next time.

The following night at dinner we again enjoyed good food, conversation, and wine, but there was no discussion of the project. I was getting very worried that we would not complete the project. I honestly do not recall whether we made a presentation at the end of the 10 days. As it turned out, the presentation was not as important as what I learned about cultural differences. A person in my group from the United Kingdom was, like me, more task oriented. French and Spanish team members, however, pointed out that they could not work with people they did not know, an idea I had never considered. The German member was equally focused on tasks and relationships. I would never have learned about the differences between task-oriented and relationship-oriented cultures and viewpoints if I had not been placed on such a multicultural team.

As an organization is expanding outside its borders of origin, it is critical to include voices from other countries and cultures. I worked for two different companies that acquired other organizations and promised to be inclusive, but then ran the business from their home country's point of view. You cannot be sensitive to colleagues from other backgrounds if they are not at the table when decisions are being made. If organizations are committed to finding ways to work together that create unique opportunities for learning, then they need to focus on representation and inclusion versus efficiency.

Adam Grant, a professor at Wharton, wrote a great book entitled, *Think Again: The Power of Knowing What You Don't Know*. Chapter 8 describes the Difficult Conversations Lab at Columbia University. People sign up to have a 20-minute conversation on a particular subject with someone they do not know and who holds a point of view regarding that subject is opposite to their own. At the end of the 20 minutes, the two people are required to sign an agreement about aspects of that subject on which they agree. Forty-six percent of the people were able to find common ground and write and sign a joint statement. The other 54% of participants were not able to agree and sign a statement about their agreements.

What are the learnings that someone could describe about what they learned? Rather than dismiss someone's ideas based on a label or a headline, be open to where you might agree and hold similar views.

In Chapter 3 of *Think Again*, Grant says that negotiators do four things better than most people: (1) They find common ground; (2) they focus on a few reasons; (3) they avoid defend/attack spirals; and (4) they ask questions. Skilled negotiators rarely go on the offensive or defensive. They express curiosity with questions like, "So you don't see any merits in that proposal at all?" As you can see, they display several of the learning agility behaviors in combination. As you attempt to work with unfamiliar colleagues from different parts of your global organization, you are going to need to use *Flexibility* to find common themes. You are going to have to use *Interpersonal Risk Taking* to surface and ask tough questions but in a way that is tough on the issue and not on the person. If, like in the Columbia Difficult Conversations Lab, your work needs to find points of agreement, it will likely lead to places never imagined.

COLLABORATING DESCRIPTOR 3: COLLABORATES WITH OTHER PARTS OF THE ORGANIZATION

One of my greatest strengths is that I am task oriented. I get things done. One of my biggest shortcomings is that I am task oriented. I sometimes look at situations to determine what I can do to be most efficient when I should be looking at being efficient and effective.

Anheuser-Busch, when I worked there, had an executive dining room. If you reached a certain level in the organization, you were entitled to free lunch. Philosophically, that did not make sense to me, and I ate elsewhere. One day, when I was working on a project and wanted my boss's input, he suggested that I come up to the dining room to discuss the issue. I went to the dining room to get his input, and also found my peers sitting around the table. I realized I was missing an opportunity to connect with them in a different way. We all had to eat lunch. Why not take advantage of this forum?

I also found out that there were "open" tables, where people who showed up at the dining room door at about the same time would be seated together. I often found myself seated with people from the engineering, marketing, international, and finance departments. We were all in St. Louis and so could talk about the Cardinals baseball team, the weather, or maybe something that was going on in our own work area. I learned new things about the business and got to know some colleagues I did not know well previously. At the time, I worked in the organization's development group, which meant that different functions asked me to work on projects for them. Sometimes I ended up at a lunch table with one of those former customers, who would mention that the project I had completed had been helpful. Sometimes that sparked the interest of another group and led to a new project. Those business opportunities might not have presented themselves without the informal lunch discussions.

Later, I moved to another role in the company where I was responsible for starting an international human resources department. I needed assistance from every part of human resources and people from different functions around the organization. Those informal lunch discussions gave me contacts and established relationships that facilitated my ability to collaborate with other parts of the organization.

Let us say you are a coach. How could you help learners develop their capability to collaborate with other parts of their organization? Their Burke assessment results would provide a baseline of their capability. They could approach *Collaborating* by specific projects or types of work they do. You could ask them to develop a list of their contacts. If the list is organized by project or type of work a group does, what individuals or groups might be a resource? If they identify a part of their work where they have no connections, that might be a gap to address. If the list is organized by functional group or business and there are sections with no contacts, they might want to look to establish a connection in those areas.

There is always a quid pro quo in these relationships. If someone is seen as a resource, people may be more inclined to provide them with assistance in the future. I love doing things for others and knowing "they owe me." It makes using the *Interpersonal Risk Taking* behavior of "asking for help" that much easier in the future.

COLLABORATING DESCRIPTOR 4: ASKS STAKEHOLDERS FOR THEIR POINT OF VIEW

When I Googled "stakeholder," the definition I found stated that a stakeholder can be either internal or external. A stakeholder is anyone affected by a business or who affects a business. Consider that idea as applied to our overall definition of *Collaborating*, which requires finding ways to work with others that generate unique opportunities for learning.

If I were trying to demonstrate this capability on a project, I would develop a list of all my internal stakeholders. I would make two columns on my internals list. In column one, I would list the internal groups my work or my group's work affects. Column two would list all the internals who affect me or my group's work. I would develop a similar list of external stakeholders who my work affects and who affect me or my work.

Next, I would prioritize each stakeholder as low, medium, or high in terms of affect. Then I would determine which stakeholder represents the greatest learning opportunity for our group. I could use low, medium, or high to categorize the learning opportunity. I might not be able to determine what the learning opportunity would be from some stakeholders. I would need to figure that out.

The Collaborating dimension of learning agility is about people and relationships and being intentional in that part of your work and life. Some of the behaviors take some time to develop. Once established, with a little ongoing nurturance, those relationships and networks can pay dividends for a lifetime.

CHAPTER 11

INFORMATION GATHERING

The Burke definition of Information Gathering *is
"Using various methods to remain current in one's field."*

Clearly, every day the amount of information being generated is increasing exponentially. The total data captured, copied, and consumed in 2020 was 64.2 zettabytes. This is compared to 2 zettabytes in 2010. (Holst, 2021). The mediums on which that information is being provided is staggering, and it is hard to stay current. Each year there are between 600,000 and 1,000,000 new books published in the U.S. alone (Morgan, 2013). Not only that, but the mediums that different generations use to obtain their information are not the same. A colleague recently said, "If I cannot put my hands on it and turn the pages with my fingers, it is not a book." I have three adult sons and I rarely see them with a book in their hands. Their main source of information is their cell phones.

Acknowledging those differences, Burke's research found four ways that a more learning agile person gathers information; they are the following:

1. Seeks new information on topics related to their field
2. Updates knowledge through training and education
3. Reads journals, books, etc. to stay informed
4. Collects data to increase knowledge and inform next steps

INFORMATION GATHERING DESCRIPTOR 1: SEEKS NEW INFORMATION ON TOPICS RELATED TO THEIR FIELD

Information Gathering in learning agility, as in life, revolves around a few basic questions: what, who, and how. Let us start with *what*. If you are gathering information on a subject that has been around for a while, you can consult books written on the subject. If the subject is more current, you may need to use Google or another search mechanism to begin the process. The topic may also affect *how* you go about seeking information. Do you know someone you consider to be an expert on the subject? You could use the *Collaborating* behavior of leveraging the skills, knowledge, and talents of experts to help you understand and sharpen your focus on the subject. They may be able to refer you to other experts or groups that focus on your topic as well as to other (collaboration) source material or search engines or descriptors.

Demonstrating this first behavior requires networking to identify people or places where you can find this content or related information. Each time you identify a new expert or another pocket of information, it can lead you in a new or expanded direction. When you keep encountering the same names and resources, it is generally an indication that you are on the diminishing-returns side of *Information Gathering*.

INFORMATION GATHERING DESCRIPTOR 2: UPDATES KNOWLEDGE THROUGH TRAINING AND EDUCATION

This area of development for increasing learning agility has changed drastically in recent years. The medium of the learning is the *how*. Traditionally, it meant in-person learning—sitting in a room with other learners and an instructor. That option still exists, and may be the best one, depending on factors such as what you need to learn and the amount of time needed or available to cover the topic. Another consideration is whether your learning requires interacting with other participants. Once you consider those factors, you should determine whether your learning can be accomplished synchronously or asynchronously. When training and education move online, you can access information from podcasts, blogs, chats, and more. Seeing others' faces, breaking into small group, and showing slides and videos can all be done virtually.

The bigger challenge may be *what* you need to learn. If you are being promoted from an individual contributor to a manager position, a coach may help you determine which leadership skills you need to develop. Leadership is a broad area; what needs to be done first, second, etc.? Who are the best providers? You could use the *Feedback Seeking* dimension to ask your manager or other people you know and respect to help you determine what you need to do to improve. You also could use the behavior from the *Collaborating* dimension of leveraging knowledge, as well as the *Interpersonal Risk Taking* dimension to talk with colleagues about mistakes or failures on previous projects.

The most important part of updating your knowledge through training and education is determining where your starting point is in a specific area, from novice to expert. The Burke Learning Agility score on this item is a starting point. You will also need a plan that includes *what* (what you will do), *how* (how you will do it) and a *when* (completion date).

INFORMATION GATHERING DESCRIPTOR 3: READS JOURNALS, BOOKS, ETC. TO STAY INFORMED

This is one of the behaviors that differentiates people who are more learning agile from those who are less so. It does indicate a bias toward using printed resources to stay current in your field, that is, how much do you read (i.e. journals, books, etc.) to stay informed.

What is stated are printed examples. The "etc." is intended to include any other way someone would access information. Books and journals tend to be more "mainstream" sources of information. Journals are a collection of related research on a subject that is overseen by a recognized expert who serves as an editor. If you need to know about current research in your field, you will typically find it in journals. There is an assumption, however, at least with journals, that the learner is familiar with those resources. If you are not, you should use the *Collaborating* dimension to ask colleagues for the names of important and respected journals or websites.

Belonging to professional societies in your field also can help expose you to new work in your area of expertise. These groups often have monthly luncheons, newsletters, and annual conferences where emerging topics are discussed.

Most people initially develop an area of expertise as their major in college. College is where you'll learn a substantial amount, but in all honesty, five years after graduation most of that information will be obsolete. If your major is technology, the obsolescence occurs in even less time. Staying current requires effort. It has been said that a person needs to spend at least 2% of their time on professional development each year. That works out to about 5 days of "work time" each year.

Any effort to improve in *Information Gathering* could start by reviewing your Burke assessment results for this dimension. The next step would be to develop a network of professional colleagues who are willing to share what they are reading or what they have heard will be the next "big idea" in their field. You will know your capability in this area is increasing when you realize you are already at least somewhat aware or knowledgeable of their answers.

Another way to improve in this area is to create a formal personal development plan for the next 12 months. Years ago, when most performance appraisals were on paper, this plan was where learners would list the courses or training programs they would participate in for professional development. This is still a useful exercise to ensure personal accountability.

In his book *Bootstrap Leadership*, Steve Arneson described creating a personal board of directors for development purposes composed of respected experts in the learner's fields. The learner commits to speak with them quarterly to get their input about what is going on in their field. This informal board can help the learner gauge how current they are in their field. If the learner is aware of the books and studies mentioned by their board of directors, we would say the individual is capable. When learners start bringing new books and studies to their board members, it would indicate that their capabilities have reached the highest end of the scale.

INFORMATION GATHERING DESCRIPTOR 4: COLLECTS DATA TO INCREASE KNOWLEDGE AND INFORM NEXT STEPS

Wikipedia defines data as a unit of information. It also describes data as something that is transformed into information when viewed in context or after being analyzed. Merriam-Webster says that data are factual information, such as measurements or statistics that are used as the basis for reasoning, discussion, or calculations. Wikipedia also says that data are used in scientific research or in business management/analysis, for example, in sales, revenue, profits, and financing. Data can help an organization determine things such as salary increases, turnover rates, productivity, and competitiveness.

In the business world, we collect information that will increase what we know about something and that will help us determine what to do next, such as determining merit pay budgets. Bits and pieces of information on inflation rates, sales projections, raw material costs, transportation costs, and interest rates are all used to determine salaries for the following year. Companies try to obtain information about competitors, the industry, and the overall economy. Then they determine who they compete with for talent, who hires employees away from them, and whether they want to pay at-market or above-market pay rates. There are no right or wrong answers. These are decisions that require data.

A FEW MORE THOUGHTS ON *INFORMATION GATHERING*

Learning agility is about having the ability to figure out what to do in situations where you have never been before. *Information Gathering* allows you to choose an area in which you want to become more proficient. Work can begin by writing out a plan of the activities you will undertake, milestones, and due dates. In the beginning, you can tap your network of experts to gain information. After you have done enough background work, you may develop your own ideas that you want to explore or different approaches you want to try (*Experimenting*). When people start coming to you as the resource or expert, you will know you are at the higher end of capability on this dimension.

CHAPTER 12

FEEDBACK SEEKING

The Burke definition of Feedback Seeking *is
"Asking others for feedback on one's ideas and overall performance."*

*F*eedback Seeking seems to be a topic most people are familiar with. It is covered in Management 101 classes and most performance appraisal training. As my colleagues and I worked with different versions of the Burke assessments and implemented them in different organizations, it became clearer that developing *Feedback Seeking* as a capability in individuals and organizations is not so simple.

Here are a few illustrations. I once worked with a leader from a pharmaceutical company to assess 150 people in one of its divisions. Everyone received their individual Burke results, and we created a composite for the entire group. The group's results were slightly below the 50th percentile. In a perfect world, I would expect a normal distribution where the average was at the 50th percentile. These results, while a little lower, should not have been a cause for great concern.

The leader, however, was very worried that the participants would have a strong negative reaction to learning that they might be below average on anything. I challenged the leader's concerns about the group's data. While their organization had a history of success, a record of success does not necessarily translate into higher learning agility. In this case, I was concerned about how this group receives feedback. If the expectation is that the group (and therefore the individuals) will be above average, that would likely start the discussion on a more defensive tone.

My second example is about someone I worked with who was responsible for innovation at a healthcare organization. On the Burke self-rated LAI, the person self-rated as above the 95th percentile overall and on every dimension. Their boss was asked to complete the Burke LAS 180 and rated them at the 50th percentile overall, with some dimensions with high scores and others with low scores. I was present when they met to discuss the results. The person assumed that the boss's low ratings were a result of input from his peers, but the boss indicated that the ratings had been their own. A potentially complicated discussion immediately became more difficult.

From a seeking feedback perspective, this person had made up their mind about the ratings with an attitude of "don't confuse me with the facts." This experience made me realize there may be an opportunity to assist people in *Feedback Seeking*, and it was certainly a larger opportunity than I had originally believed.

The definition of *Feedback Seeking* is "Asking others for feedback on one's ideas and overall performance." A person who is more learning agile demonstrates *Feedback Seeking* in these ways:

1. Asks peers for feedback on performance
2. Seeks feedback from manager
3. Discusses potential advancement with manager
4. Asks others how to improve performance

This chapter will look at these behavioral statements and discuss how you can develop increased capability in each of these four areas. Most often feedback is something that is given by a supervisor to a learner. As the items are written in the Burke inventory, it is the learners who are initiating conversations about their performance with their supervisors. They are asking how they are doing in general and then in terms of their advancement potential. The other two feedback requests are being made to peers and then "others" in general.

SEEKING FEEDBACK FROM OTHERS

This section applies to all four items in this dimension and to seeking feedback no matter the source. The nuance in descriptor 3 about seeking feedback related to advancement will be addressed separately. But first some questions: How can you "set the stage" for obtaining feedback? Are there better ways of asking for feedback? How do you help "others," including your supervisor, peers, and other colleagues, give feedback in a helpful way after you ask for it? You also need to examine how you take in and use the information you receive. If these interactions are going to lead to growth and development, they are going to have to be happening over time. How will you create an environment that promotes constructive feedback that becomes the catalyst for personal development over time?

Many times, leaders give feedback only when there is a performance problem. This chapter is discussing feedback being exchanged to help learners improve. A learner may have volunteered for a challenging project or may have agreed to participate even though the outcome is unknown or ambiguous. Feedback conversations should be focused on *what* happened and *how* everyone can improve.

Self-awareness also is an important part of asking for and receiving feedback. How well do you know yourself? Internal self-awareness means gaining insight by looking inward; external self-awareness means turning your gaze outward to understand how you are seen. For most people, learning how others see you is usually thwarted by one single fact: Even the people you are closest to are often reluctant to share such information.

Once the feedback seeker gets another person to agree to give the feedback, a major obstacle has been overcome. As a refresher, let us review some basic guidelines for the feedback giver, as often feedback givers are not skilled at this role. Just because someone is an experienced supervisor does not necessarily mean they are skilled at giving feedback. In a perfect situation, a coach would work both sides of this dynamic (feedback provider/supervisor and feedback receiver)—working with the supervisor to prepare them to give feedback effectively and with the employee to prepare them to receive feedback effectively. Ideally, a coach would facilitate a few early feedback discussions to ensure their effectiveness. There may be instances where the feedback receiver needs to help the giver to allow them to get what they need to improve. Here are some tips for feedback givers to improve their interactions:

- Be prepared (do not wing it).
- Offer feedback soon after the situation occurs (timely).
- Provide specifics.
- Describe what happened behaviorally (what the person did).
  - What did the person do effectively?
  - What does the person need to do or do differently?

- Ask the feedback receiver to paraphrase what they heard in the previous step (do not move on until what the feedback giver said is what the receiver heard).
- Determine the next steps (ideally this will be described by the employee; this needs to be a dialogue so if the feedback provider/supervisor does not agree with the next steps, they can describe what they are concerned about). This does not need to be a finished plan. The objective here is for the receiver/employee to receive and understand feedback from the feedback provider/supervisor. Part of ensuring that feedback is clear is discovering how the employee will put the feedback into action going forward.
- Create scales for the feedback giver and receiver to rate their interaction in terms of understanding the feedback given, whether the feedback receiver felt listened to and heard, and clarity of next steps. The supervisor/feedback provider and learner/feedback receiver should independently rate their experiences during the feedback session and discuss ratings that differ by more than one point.

UNDERSTOOD

The category being measured is "Understanding." Understanding is something in a person's head. The way to take this invisible concept of Understanding and make it visible or concrete is to have the person articulate what they "see." Once the feedback giver can see what the feedback receiver "understood" as demonstrated by their description of what they "saw," the feedback giver can modify their description to increase the feedback receiver's "Understood."

Unclear How What I Did Was Seen	Some Parts of What I Did Were Clear and Others Not	Extremely Clear How What I Did Was Seen
1 2	3 4 5	6 7

HEARD

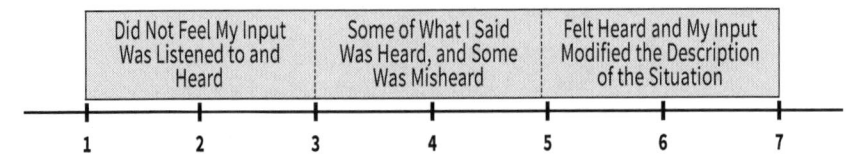

| Did Not Feel My Input Was Listened to and Heard | Some of What I Said Was Heard, and Some Was Misheard | Felt Heard and My Input Modified the Description of the Situation |

1　　2　　3　　4　　5　　6　　7

CLARITY OF NEXT STEPS

| Do Not Understand What I Need to Improve | Some Steps Are Clear and Others Are Unclear | Extremely Clear What Steps I Need to Take to Improve |

1　　2　　3　　4　　5　　6　　7

This rating scale could be shared with the feedback giver when discussing how to improve feedback giving to prepare both people in the exchange for how each can help the other.

On the other side of the feedback discussion is the person who is receiving the feedback. To improve interactions, the feedback receiver should:

- Be appreciative. Giving feedback involves work on the part of the feedback giver. Feedback is a gift. Really.
- Listen to understand. Some people call this active listening. The feedback receiver needs to demonstrate that what the feedback giver is saying is what the receiver is hearing. It is OK to ask questions to clarify what was heard. The objective as the feedback giver is to understand how what they said was heard and experienced by the feedback receiver.
- Leave any defensiveness at home. The feedback receiver may not like what they are hearing. If the feedback receiver puts the giver on the spot, the conversation will be over.

- Be clear about next steps. Let us assume that there are three to five actions or deliverables coming out of the feedback discussion. A completed plan is not necessary, but the feedback receiver should know and agree on what the deliverables are and for whom, the general time frame, and the deadline for finishing the work.

We talked about the feedback receiver and the manager/feedback giver rating their feedback session on understanding the feedback, feeling heard, and being clear on next steps. Assuming these steps are part of a longer-term development relationship, their working relationship should improve over time.

The nature of *what* the employee is working on may make a feedback session more challenging. Feedback can be critical and surprising. Sometimes it can be critical and confusing, which means it supports a weakness the employee is aware of (Eurich, 2017, p. 180). For example, let's say the person has been told previously that they are defensive when under pressure. In this situation, the person is told they were being defensive. An uncomfortable feedback session does not mean that progress was not made. It may feel like a temporary setback, but if the employee and the feedback provider continue to talk about their relationship and the specific issues that arise, the relationship should get back on track fairly quickly.

Tasha Eurich, in her book *Insight*, says, "If we can receive feedback with grace, reflect on it with courage and respond to it with purpose, we are capable of unearthing unimaginable insights from the most unlikely of places" (2017, p. 180). Eurich describes a technique called self-affirmation, which can be used to make difficult feedback easier to hear. Before receiving the feedback, the receiver should focus on a positive aspect of themselves. This makes them more open to hearing difficult feedback. This technique is similar to the Burke *Flexibility* dimension of changing the framework. Here is an example of having an advancement discussion with your supervisor.

FEEDBACK SEEKING DESCRIPTOR 3: DISCUSSING ADVANCEMENT WITH YOUR SUPERVISOR

First, why would you have a discussion about advancement with your boss? Maybe your next move in the organization is to your boss's job. If that is the case, it is likely that your boss will significantly impact the decision of whether to give you that role, so shouldn't their input be sought? Ensuring your boss sees your strengths and development areas will be important to gaining their support as that decision is being made. Your boss and your boss's boss are likely having ongoing discussions about your boss's successor, evaluating each candidate, their development needs, and whether that development is happening. An interesting aside is that at your current level, you may be looking at your boss and thinking, "I could do what they do as well or better than they can." Maybe so. However, your view of your boss's world is from your perspective. The air is very different at that next level, and that is difficult to understand until you are sitting in that chair.

You may still be questioning why you need to have an advancement conversation with your boss, particularly if in your next role you would be moving to another division, function, or even country. Your candidacy for another role is based on your current performance and that of your team. Any potential new boss will ask your current boss for feedback on your strengths, any concerns about you in your current role, and any development areas they might see for you in the new role. Your current boss can make all the difference whether that conversation goes any further. One more issue to consider related to potential advancement is whether you have a successor for your current role. You may have difficulty getting the feedback you seek if your boss fears the effect your departure would create. In short, think in advance about finding your successor as you prepare to talk about your advancement.

So now you are ready to open Pandora's box by having a conversation about your advancement with your boss. Make sure you schedule the conversation at a time of year and a time of day when neither of you is "under the gun" about something. The tone of this conversation needs to be relaxed and unrushed. Make sure your boss understands that your expectations are that this change is not imminent, but that you two need to talk about the future, and you have taken the initiative to start the conversation.

Your boss is either going to be helpful or not. You know your boss, so you will have a pretty good idea which way it will go. Either way, you need to be prepared. If your boss is going to be of no help, then you are going to have to "manage up" and be the energy that moves things along. I have seen unhelpful bosses take two forms. In one, your boss is clueless, and you will have to create and facilitate the agenda. In the other, your boss will say, "Everything is great." That is flattering, but everyone has aspects of themselves that can be improved. Neither one of those responses gives you much to work with.

You have a few options. You could request a new assessment or ask to use your latest performance review. Let me endorse multi-rater feedback. In *Insight*, Eurich includes a quote from Marcus Aurelius: "Everything we hear is an opinion and not a fact." Eurich goes on to say that "a good rule of thumb is feedback from one person is a perception; feedback from two people is a pattern; but feedback from three or more people is as likely to as close to a fact as you can get" (p. 179). The Burke LAS 180 or 360 would be a source for feedback from your boss. On most performance appraisal forms, the last page is for development. Either one of those sources would give you content to discuss.

With a Burke survey, you would have a quantitative starting point. For example, you could look at the *Flexibility* dimension. Suppose there is a difference between your rating and your boss's rating. More specifically, the first area of *proposes innovative solutions* is the biggest gap. Your boss rated you as a 3, and you rated yourself as a 6. What were the things your boss saw or did not see that caused them to rate you as a 3? Hopefully, talking about the issue with greater specificity will lead to a greater appreciation for each other's perspective. Your next question should be, "What does a 6 or 7 look like?" Assuming your boss can articulate that, a next step could be to pick a project or assignment that you are already doing or could do where you would have a chance to demonstrate those 6 and 7 behaviors and results.

You need to create a plan with measurable milestones and due dates that you both will sign off on. You also need to set the date for your next meeting or check-in. Do not let more than a month go by before meeting again. Ideally, you would schedule the next meeting around a milestone so there would be some tangible results to discuss.

If the source document for this conversation is the performance appraisal and the development plan, then you need to add measurability. Let us assume the development plan includes gaining cross-functional experience. You and your boss must determine the following:

- What is the cross-functional project going to be?
- What are the outcomes if you are successful?
- Who will be included on the project?
- What is the developmental capability you must demonstrate?
- How is that capability related to your future promotability?

Both you and boss should rate your starting point on a scale of 1 to 7. Where are you now? What would a 7 look like? You need to define and have a shared understanding of the target. Then the process again needs a plan, milestones, due dates, and date and agenda for the next meeting.

When you have a boss who is helpful, many of these issues are nonexistent or much easier to handle. The area to look out for is a plan with specificity and measurability, and follow-up meetings. You should focus on gaining the advocacy of your boss around future advancement. One measure of success would be advancement.

FEEDBACK SEEKING DESCRIPTOR 1: ASKS PEERS FOR FEEDBACK ON PERFORMANCE AND DESCRIPTOR 4: ASKS OTHERS HOW TO IMPROVE PERFORMANCE

The two remaining items in the *Feedback Seeking* dimension are *Asks peers for feedback on performance* and *Asks others how to improve performance*. Technically, peers are an "other." I use peers in this section knowing everything also applies to any other "others." The focus on performance can mean one or both of two things: what and how. The results, or *what* was done, should be straightforward; results should speak for themselves. If there was no agreement on the target at the beginning, then a shared understanding of and commitment to the target must be created.

Assuming the target is clear, then the performance feedback conversation should focus on the means, or *how* the results were accomplished.

These "how" measures need to be determined and implemented on the next project. Leaders require frequent check-ins and need to monitor how the feedback seeker is doing and make corrections if things are not on target. If Burke LAS 360 results are available, the leader should use the peers perspective for a baseline, then determine improvement goals and plans.

The "asking others" aspect of how to improve performance could be based on Burke LAS 360 results. The "others" group can be whoever's feedback would help the leader improve their learning agility. The Burke LAS 360 data give nine categories and 38 items to use as a starting point to improve learning agility. If Burke 360 data are not available, you can go back to two standard questions: What did the leader do well on this project or in this area, and what does the leader need to do better, do differently, or start doing? On a scale of 1 to 7, ask others to rate where the leader is now. The leader should also rate themselves in this area.

A FEW MORE THOUGHTS ON *FEEDBACK SEEKING*

Feedback Seeking is one of the easier learning agility dimensions to develop. It does require courage to ask for feedback and persistence and patience to work through the specificity of *what* and *how*. The breakthroughs are exhilarating and fuel deeper, more rewarding conversations. I do want to acknowledge that there may be things the leader cannot or will not change. Eurich in *Insight* suggests making that explicit and asking others for help in working around it (pp. 186–187).

Steve Arneson's book *Bootstrap Leadership* was referenced in the chapter on *Information Gathering*. It is also a useful resource for developing learning agility in *Feedback Seeking*. The book consists of 50 short chapters that are all related to improving as a leader. Only one is about feedback, and it is entitled "What the Boss Needs to Hear." That title is also related to the dimension *Flexibility*: "Being open to new ideas and proposing new solutions." This represents the basics of seeking and using feedback to improve learning agility. Several other learning agility dimensions and behaviors can be used along with *Feedback Seeking* to deepen a person's skill level, such as aspects of *Speed*. For example, in the IT software development area, "sprints" are short, all-out bursts to make rapid progress in an area that also involve aspects of *Experimenting*, such as learning by trial and error or trying new ways to solve problems.

You could intersperse these approaches with a feedback loop or series of loops to improve performance. With *Performance Risk Taking*, you could take on risky or ambiguous work and ask for frequent and specific feedback to make sure you do not get too far off track. Using *Interpersonal Risk Taking* could help you surface and address tough issues, discuss mistakes, and ask for help. *Feedback Seeking* would help with every aspect of *Collaborating*. *Information Gathering* could be used to update your knowledge related to the feedback received and to then collect more information. *Reflecting* should always be part of your *Feedback Seeking* process; you should always be thinking about how to be more effective. That is the dimension we will examine next.

CHAPTER 13

REFLECTING

The Burke definition of Reflecting *is
"Slowing down to evaluate one's own performance to be more effective."*

Reflecting is often considered the ninth dimension of learning agility, even though there is no strict numerical sequence to the dimensions. *Reflecting* may be something you do after completing an activity to determine what went well and what could be improved. It could also be what you do as the precursor to a set of actions. *Reflecting* after an activity has occurred can be the first step in a future planning process.

Years ago, I was exposed to the Deming cycle of continuous process improvement. This model, created by William Edwards Deming, has four steps: Plan, Do, Study, and Act. *Reflecting* occurs at the end of an improvement cycle and is the first step in the planning component of a subsequent cycle. However, many individuals follow a process of Plan, Do, Plan, Do, Plan, Do. This was evident with one leadership group I worked with in reviewing their composite Burke LAI results. The group's lowest score was on *Reflecting*, and they didn't disagree with the rating.

We talked about what a lack of *Reflecting* looked like in their day-to-day activities; next, members of the group were to write down in journals what they had learned and some potential action steps for improvement. About 5 minutes into this activity, I noticed conversations starting and phones coming out and texts being sent. I pointed out to the group what I witnessed: When they were given an opportunity for *Reflecting*, they reverted to do, do, do. *Reflecting* was not part of their normal routine, and they did not take advantage of the opportunity when it was given to them.

Burke in his research found that a person who is higher in *Reflecting* demonstrates this capability in four different ways:

1. Reflects on work processes and projects
2. Reflects on how to be more effective
3. Considers reasons for and consequences of actions or events
4. Evaluates events with others to understand what happened

REFLECTING DESCRIPTOR 1: REFLECTS ON WORK PROCESSES AND PROJECTS

The two elements in this first behavior of *Reflecting* are the *what* and the *how* of completing a project. Suppose you are in the role of a coach. In looking retrospectively at a project, you want to answer two questions.

First, what went well? You might want to drill down further and answer the who, what, and why of what went well to capture the learnings for posterity. It is important to build on learnings and reflections, and duplicate and improve on what was done well on future projects. You need to be specific about all the elements that went well. Spend time looking for connections or patterns that emerge. Here you are demonstrating one of the behaviors from the *Flexibility* dimension, *finds common themes*. Being able to summarize what was done on a project in a way that has not been done before could have implications for future work.

Second, what went well on the project from a process perspective? This is standard process improvement practice, as referenced earlier with the Deming cycle and its four steps of Plan, Do, Study, and Act. You want to be able to articulate what the process was, with a flowchart of the steps so that they can be replicated consistently. If deviations in the process occurred, what are they? What needs to be done to get the process consistent again?

Go through the same evaluation of *what* and *how* for the problem areas on the project. You and the learner could potentially learn as much from analyzing difficulties as from analyzing successes. This may provide an opportunity to look at the behaviors under *Experimenting*, which is explained in an earlier chapter. If some things are identified as problematic in a past project, the learner may want to make changes in the future to remediate those problems. Another opportunity is to use the behaviors from *Interpersonal Risk Taking* of *brings up tough issues with others* and *discusses mistakes with others*. You may need to make explicit that the objective is learning, not assigning blame; the situation needs to be made psychologically "safe" to be able to discuss what happened and what needs to be improved. If the discussion becomes personal, it will essentially be over. If the learner can follow that principle, you can have a content-rich discussion. Before ending the discussion, use the *Flexibility* behavior of trying to find themes or connections.

REFLECTING DESCRIPTOR 2: REFLECTS ON HOW TO BE MORE EFFECTIVE

Reflecting is a critical behavior that requires taking time on a regular basis for both retrospective and prospective reflection. Take 5 to 10 minutes every morning or evening to do the thinking required. Write it down so your insights and learnings are not lost. Do the same thing on a weekly basis, spending 15 minutes as you are winding down on Friday afternoon or 15 minutes on Sunday night as you begin to think about the week ahead. Having a plan will give you focus, but it will be even better if it is in the context of being more effective. For example, when I coach leaders on *Reflecting*, I ask them to both prepare for and review the results of team meetings to determine what went well and what could have been better. What if the leader approached the pre- and post-team meetings with the goal of executing a specific leadership style and getting a team to use specific learning agility behaviors? The coach would be part of the process. The "leader" announces to their coach that they want to work on their leadership style and certain learning agility behaviors. The leader then creates a plan to address these issues with their staff. The coach assists and provides input to the leader around the leader's goals regarding leadership style and learning agility behaviors.

The leader conducts the meeting. In the post-meeting the leader gets feedback at least from their coach. The coach also asks the leader to rate their own performance. This would allow the leader to reflect both generally and specifically on how to be more effective in terms of their own leadership style and learning agility behaviors.

REFLECTING DESCRIPTOR 3: CONSIDERS REASONS FOR AND CONSEQUENCES OF ACTIONS OR EVENTS

There are two parts to this behavior: the *why*, or reasons for something, and the result of what happened. Being able to describe the reasons for something requires a great deal of self-awareness. While we believe there is a relationship between learning agility and self-awareness, we do not have any data to support that assertion.

I talked about self-awareness in the preceding chapter on *Feedback Seeking*. The idea is the better you know yourself, the better you can objectively describe why you did what you did. Another resource is others and using the *Feedback Seeking* behavior of *asks others how to improve performance*. The challenge here is twofold. The other person will describe what they saw you do, and your challenge is to hear and understand them. Any questions you might ask would be to clarify what you heard. Any response on your part that sounds defensive will be detrimental to receiving the information you are requesting. The other person can only tell you what they see; they cannot determine the *why*, or your motivation.

The other part of this behavior is the impact or consequences of actions or events. Here are two examples. Suppose you are a leader who has just publicly praised one of your employees. Ten minutes later, you ask for volunteers to take on a difficult assignment, and the employee you just praised steps up. Let us assume the employee volunteering is a consequence of the earlier praising. In a second situation, you hold a staff meeting where you ask for feedback, but there is little discussion. One of your peers who attended the meeting tells you that every time you introduce a subject and ask for feedback, you give your opinion early on. Your peer suggests that if you withheld your own opinion, you would get more feedback. That solution might require you to use the *Interpersonal Risk-Taking* behavior of *asks others for help*. You could solicit help from one of the more senior members of your team; when a subject is opened for discussion, your volunteer could signal for you to be quiet or ask you to hold your thoughts until later.

This provides two examples of addressing the *what* and the consequences it can have. Working on that specific issue allows you to make progress in one area. Taking a bigger perspective approach would be to find out, how your team rates on overall effectiveness on a scale of 1 to 7. The team could continue to discuss individual and group issues as it relates to overall team effectiveness. Continuing to take periodic measures would allow the team to measure improvement over time.

REFLECTING DESCRIPTOR 4: EVALUATES EVENTS WITH OTHERS TO UNDERSTAND WHAT HAPPENED

Any postmortem on an event should include a discussion with the people involved. Two questions should be answered: What went well, and what could have been done better? A subset of question 2 could be, What could the group have done that it did not do, and why didn't it happen? As the leader, you should focus on things that went well as well as areas needing improvement. Record the group's observations on a whiteboard or a laptop to ensure three things: suggestions aren't lost, comments aren't repeated, and input can spark discussion on new ideas.

Next, create a document that summarizes all the reflections on the event. If conducting this kind of postmortem is a new activity for you, consider using a trained facilitator who has no investment in the content to ask questions and record what they hear. It is hard for a leader of a team to simultaneously facilitate the discussion, record the comments, and make comments.

There is an opportunity to use behaviors from two other dimensions while carrying out this activity.

Interpersonal Risk Taking

1. Brings up tough issues with others
2. Asks others for help
3. Discusses mistakes with others
4. Challenges others' ideas even when they are shared by many

Collaborating

1. Leverages skills, knowledge, and talents of others
2. Works with colleagues of different backgrounds
3. Collaborates with other parts of the organization
4. Asks stakeholders for their point of view

As the leader, you might decide to conduct more than one postmortem session. You could do one with the people who worked directly on the project, then hold a separate session with stakeholders to determine how satisfied they were. If there is another group in the organization that is better at this activity than the group being worked with, you could seek the critique of this more effective group. The output of the postmortems is intended to capture strengths to be continued and improved.

A FEW MORE THOUGHTS ON *REFLECTING*

Improvement areas are opportunities to increase capability on the next event or activity. They need to be assigned to a learner, and what they are going to improve and when should be defined. During the next event, in the planning phase *Reflecting* will be the starting point. This process should be repeated at the end of every subsequent activity. This may seem counterintuitive, but sometimes a learner needs to go slow to go fast. *Reflecting* represents slowing down, the output of which will allow progress to occur more quickly.

EPILOGUE

This learning agility journey began 30 years ago when it was apparent that while existing assessment tools to identify and develop talent were good, they were just not good enough. The success rate in identifying the best talent was around 50%, which meant there were almost an equal number of failures. Talent development professionals in big companies knew there was an "X factor" that had not been defined, a factor that would bring the ability to predict success to a higher level. Burke, along with several of his doctoral students at Columbia University, dug into the existing research, confirmed it, and expanded it. Five years later, Burke had good, solid data concerning 38 items that defined and measured the construct of learning agility.

Those items then needed to be translated into an assessment tool, a means to evaluate people against those items. The initial self-assessment was expanded to include two multi-rater versions. A means of transferring this capability to others was needed and a certification process was created. Learning agility as a concept was showing up in a variety of forms, some more sophisticated than others. To shape the conversation around learning agility Hoff and Burke wrote *Learning Agility: The Key to Leader Potential*. They wanted an opportunity to define learning agility, starting with the research, and including the research. They wanted to demonstrate to potential users of these assessments how they could be applied to every human resource system, from selection to succession.

Entropy is the natural running down of an organization. The same is true with a construct like learning agility. You are only as good as the last contribution to this area. The initial Burke data were normed in 2016. While the data were groundbreaking, they described only a U.S.-based population. Subsequently, data were collected from other parts of the world, and a 2018 re-normed set of data included a population breakdown of

50% from the United States and 50% from outside the United States. The 2018 norm group consisted of middle and senior level managers. A customer request led to an opportunity to expand the 2018 sample to include individual contributors. There were not any significant differences in the individual contributor population, but now there were data to support that statement empirically.

People were asking about the relationship between personality and learning agility. We thought there were connections but had no data to support our beliefs. We then worked with Hogan Assessments to provide a data-based response. First of all, a person's personality is fixed (difficult to change) by age 20. Learning agility, on the other hand, is behaviorally based and therefore changeable. The connections we did find was that learning agility, as defined by Burke, positively correlated with the Big 5 dimensions of Agreeableness, Conscientiousness, and Openness to Experiences. Similarly, there was a negative correlation between learning agility and the dimensions of Neuroticism and External Locus of Control. The other finding of note was a strong correlation between Burke's Overall Learning Agility scores and Hogan's Openness to New Experiences and Inquisitiveness. There is also a strong relationship between Burke's Flexibility dimension and Hogan's Openness to New Experiences. None of these relationships was surprising, more confirming what we believed to be true.

The most important question that can be asked about an assessment tool is: Does it predict success? Finding the answer to this question is a long road. To date, we have performed three studies that have demonstrated in a statistically significant way that people who score higher on the Burke LAI are seen as better performers.

Our hope with this book was to provide an update on the state of Burke's learning agility. The number of tools available to assess learning agility has grown, and we tried to provide guidance in that regard. The biggest contribution this book can make to the area of learning agility is to show people how learning agility can be developed. If organizations are going to benefit from assessing their employees, the next step is to improve what needs development.

What other work is unfinished related to learning agility? We are currently looking at our existing data on cognitive ability and learning agility. It will be interesting to see if our hypotheses are correct about any relationships. The relationship between learning agility and emotional intelligence is also an area that needs to be studied. We hope to begin that research in 2022.

Translating the Burke assessments into other languages is another recent focus. We recently completed a Spanish version, and work is underway to translate the first book into Spanish which should lead to other opportunities. A collaborator in Holland has translated the Burke items into 15 different European languages.

Another frontier is measuring the learning agility of groups and teams. This is not a question of assessing individuals who work together and creating a group profile—that is an arithmetic summary of the individuals, not their collective agility. We hope to have results in this area by the end of 2022.

This is a journey and not a destination. We appreciate your joining us and pushing us, and we welcome your feedback.

REFERENCES

American Educational Research Association, American Psychological Association, & National Council on Measurement in Education. (2014). *Standards for educational and psychological testing*. American Educational Research Association.

Anderson, J. C., & Gerbing, D. W. (1988). Structural equation modeling in practice: A review and recommended two-step approach. *Psychological Bulletin, 103*, 411–423.

Argyris, C. (1985). *Strategy, change and defensive routines*. Pitman.

Argyris, C. (1993). *Knowledge for action: Changing the status quo*. Jossey-Bass.

Argyris, C., & Schön, D. A. (1996). *Organization learning II*. Addison-Wesley.

Arneson, S. (2010). *Bootstrap leadership: 50 ways to break out, take charge and move up*. Berrett-Koehler.

Bandura, A. (1977). Self-efficacy: Toward a unifying theory of behavioral change. *Psychological Review, 84*(2), 191.

Bergh, D. (2015). Sample size and chi-squared test of fit—A comparison between a random sample approach and a chi-square value adjustment method using Swedish adolescent data. In *Pacific Rim Objective Measurement Symposium (PROMS) 2014 Conference Proceedings* (pp. 197–211). Berlin: Springer.

Bradford, L., Gibb, J. E., & Benne, K. D. (1964). *T-group theory and laboratory method*. New York: Wiley and Sons.

Brehm, J. W. (1966). *A theory of psychological reactance*. Academic Press.

Brown, K. G., & Sitzmann, T. (2011). Training and employee development for improved performance. In S. Zedeck (Ed.), *APA handbook of industrial and organizational psychology*, Vol. 2 (pp. 469–503). American Psychological Association.

Burke LAI Standard®. (2018). E.A.S.I-Consult®, LLC.

Burke LAI Expanded Version®. (2018). E.A.S.I-Consult®, LLC.

Burke LAS 180™. (2018). E.A.S.I-Consult®, LLC.

Burke LAS 360™. (2018). E.A.S.I-Consult®, LLC.

Burke, W. W. (2016). *Burke Learning Agility Inventory technical report*. E.A.S.I-Consult®.

Burke, W. W. (2018). *Organization change: Theory and practice* (5th ed.). SAGE Publications.

Burke, W. W., & Smith, D. (2019). *Burke Learning Agility Inventory technical report v3.5*. E.A.S.I-Consult®.

Burke, W. W., Roloff, K., Mitchinson, A., Catenacci, L., Drinka., G. O., & Kim, J. (2016). To live is to learn: A behavioral model and measurement of learning agility. (Unpublished manuscript). Department of Organization & Leadership, Teachers College, Columbia University.

Cable, D. M., & Judge, T. A. (1994). Pay preferences and job search decisions: A person-organization fit perspective. *Personnel Psychology, 47*, 317–348.

Cardenas, R. (2017). *The Connection between personality traits and learning agility*. E.A.S.I.-Consult®. www.easiconsult.com

Catenacci-Francois, L. (2018). Learning agility in context: Engineers' perceptions of psychologically safe climate on performance. [Unpublished doctoral dissertation]. Columbia University.

Daniel, W. W. (1990). Spearman rank correlation coefficient. In *Applied nonparametric statistics* (2nd ed., pp. 358–365). PWS-Kent.

De Meuse, K. P. (2017). Learning agility: Its evolution as a psychological construct and its empirical relationship to leader success. *Consulting Psychology Journal: Practice and Research, 69*, 267–295.

De Meuse, K. P., Dai, G., Eichinger, R. W., Page, R. C., Clark, L. P., & Zewdie, S. (2011). *The development and validation of a self-assessment of learning agility*. [Technical report]. Minneapolis, MN: Korn/Ferry International.

Deming, W. E. (1993). *The new economics for industry, government and education*. MIT Press.

DeRue, D. S., Ashford, S. J., & Myers, C. G. (2012a). Learning agility: In search of conceptual clarity and theoretical grounding. *Industrial and Organizational Psychology, 5*(3), 258–279.

DeRue, D. S., Nahrgang, J. D., Hollenbeck, J. R., & Workman, K. (2012b). A quasi-experimental study of after-event review and leadership development. *Journal of Applied Psychology, 97*, 997–1015.

Drinka, G. A. O. (2018). *Coaching for learning agility: The importance of leader behavior, learning goal orientation, and psychological safety.* (Unpublished doctoral dissertation). Columbia University.

Dweck, C. S. (1986). Motivational processes affecting learning. *American Psychologist, 41*, 1040–1048.

Eichinger, R. W., & Lombardo, M. M. (2004). Learning agility as a prime indicator of potential. *People and Strategy, 27*(4), 12.

Elliott, E. S., & Dweck, C. S. (1988). Goals: An approach to motivation and achievement. *Journal of Personality and Social Psychology, 54*(1), 5–12. http://doi.org/10.1037/0022-3514.54.1.5

Ferris, D. L., Brown, D. J., Berry, J. W., & Lian, H. (2008). The development and validation of the Workplace Ostracism Scale. *The Journal of Applied Psychology, 93*(6), 1348–66. http://doi.org/10.1037/a0012743

Gallwey, W. T. (1974). *The inner game of tennis.* Random House.

Glick, W. H. (1985). Conceptualizing and measuring organizational and psychological climate: Pitfalls in multilevel research. *Academy of Management Review, 10*(3), 601–616.

Grant, A. (2021). *Think again: The power of knowing what you don't know.* Penguin Random House.

Helmenstine, A. M. (2020). *Independent variable definition and examples.* Thought Company.

REFERENCES

Hoff, D. F., & Burke, W. W. (2017). *Learning agility: The key to leader potential.* Hogan Press.

Hoffman, B. J., & Woehr, D. J. (2006). A quantitative review of the relationship between person–organization fit and behavioral outcomes. *Journal of Vocational Behavior, 68*(3), 389–399.

Hogan, J., Hogan, R., & Kaiser, R. B. (2009). Management derailment: Personality assessment and mitigation. In S. Zedeck (Ed.) *American Psychological Association Handbook of Industrial and Organizational Psychology* (pp. 555–575). American Psychological Association.

Hogan, R., Curphy, G. J., & Hogan, J. (1994). What we know about leadership: Effectiveness and personality. *American Psychologist, 49,* 493–504.

Holst, A. (2021, June 7). *Amount of data created, consumed, and stored 2010–2025.* Statista. https://www.statista.com/statistics/871513/worldwide-data-created/

Industry Week Staff. (2020). GM, Ventec land contentious contract to produce ventilators for US government. *Industry Week,* Apr 8.

Isaacson, W. (2017). *Leonardo da Vinci.* Simon & Schuster.

Judge, T. A., & Bono, J. E. (2001). Relationship of core self-evaluations traits—self-esteem, generalized self-efficacy, locus of control, and emotional stability—with job satisfaction and job performance: A meta-analysis. *Journal of Applied Psychology, 86*(1), 80.

Judge, T. A., Locke, E. A., & Durham, C. C. (1997). The dispositional causes of job satisfaction: A core evaluations approach. *Research in Organizational Behavior, 19,* 151–188.

Kadushin, C., Hoover, J., & Tichy, M. (1971.) How and where to find intellectual elite in the United States. *Public Opinion Quarterly, 35*(1), 1–18.

Kahneman, D. (2011). Thinking, Fast and Slow. Farrar, Straus and Giroux.

Kahneman, D., & Tversky, A. (1984). Choices, values, and frames. *American Psychologist, 39*(4), 341.

Kaiser, R. B., Hogan, R., & Craig, S. B. (2008). Leadership and the fate of organizations. *American Psychologist, 63,* 96–110.

Kashy, D. A., Wood, W., & Quinn, J. M. (2002). Habits in everyday life: Thought, emotion and action. *Journal of Personality and Social Psychology, 83*(6), 1281–1297.

Kline, R. B. (2005). *Principles and practice of structural equation modeling.* Guilford.

LePine, J. A., Colquitt, J. A., & Erez, A. (2000). Adaptability to changing task contexts: Effects of general cognitive ability, conscientiousness, and openness to experience. *Personnel Psychology, 53,* 563–593.

Lewin, K. (1936). *Principles of topological psychology.* McGraw-Hill.

Lewis, K. (2003). Measuring transactive memory systems in the field: Scale development and validation. *Journal of Applied Psychology, 88*(4), 587–604. http://doi.org/10.1037/0021-9010.88.4.587

Lombardo, M. M., & Eichinger, R. W. (2000). High potentials as high learners. *Human Resource Management, 39*(4), 321–329.

Lopes, L. L. (1987). Between hope and fear: The psychology of risk. *Advances in Experimental Social Psychology, 20,* 255–295.

MacDonald, A. P. (1970). Revised scale for ambiguity tolerance: Reliability and validity. *Psychological Reports, 26*(3), 791–798.

McCall, M. W. (2010). Recasting leadership development. *Industrial and Organizational Psychology: Perspectives on Science and Practice, 3*(1), 3–19.

McCall, M. W., Lombardo, M. M. & Morrison, A. M. (1988). *Lessons of experience: How successful executives develop on the job.* Simon and Schuster.

McCauley, C. D., Ruderman, M. N., Ohlett, P. J., & Morrow, J. E. (1994). Assessing the developmental components of managerial jobs, *Journal of Applied Psychology, 79,* 544–560.

McCrae, R. R. (2004). Openness to experience. *Encyclopedia of Applied Psychology.* Elsevier.

McKenna, R. M., Boyd T. N., & Yost, P. R. (2007). Learning agility in clergy: Understanding the personal strategies and situational factors that enable pastors to learn from experience. *Journal of Psychology and Theology, 35,* 190–201.

Mitchinson, A., & Morris, R. (2012). *Learning about learning agility.* Center for Creative Leadership.

Mitchinson, A., Gerard, N. M., Roloff, K. S., & Burke, W. W. (2012). Learning agility: Spanning the rigor–relevance divide. *Industrial and Organizational Psychology, 5*(3), 287–290.

Morgan, N. (2013, January 8). Thinking of self-publishing your book in 2013? Here is what you need to know. https://www.forbes.com/sites/nickmorgan/2013/01/08/thinking-of-self-publishing-your-book-in-2013-heres-what-you-need-to-know/?sh=218b834c14bb

Morrison, A. M., White, R. P., & Van Velsor, E. (1992). *Breaking the glass ceiling: Can women reach the top of America's largest corporations?* Basic Books.

Morrison, R. F. & Branter, T. M. (1992). What enhances or inhibits learning a new job? *Journal of Applied Psychology, 77*(6), 926.

Neal, D., Wood, W., & Quinn, J. (2006) Habits-A Repeat Performance. *Current Directions in Psychological Science, 15*(4), 198–202.

Oreg, S. (2003). Resistance to change: Developing an individual differences measure. *Journal of Applied Psychology, 88*(4), 680.

Rotter, J. B. (1966). Generalized expectancies for internal versus external control of reinforcement. *Psychological Monographs: General and Applied, 80*(1), 1.

Schön, D. A. (1983). *The reflective practitioner.* New York: Basic Books.

Schreiber, J., Nora, A., Stage, F. K., Barlow, E. A., & King, J. (2006). Reporting structural equation modeling and confirmatory factor analysis results: A review. *The Journal of Educational Research, 6*(99), 323–338. http://doi.org/10.3200/JOER.99.6.323-338

Schwarz, G. (1978). Estimating the dimension of a model. *The Annals of Statistics, 6*(2), 461–464. http://doi.org/10.1214/aos/1176344136

Seifert, C. F., Yukl, G., & McDonald, R. A. (2003). Effects of multisource feedback and a feedback facilitator on the influence behavior of managers toward subordinates, *Journal of Applied Psychology, 88,* 561–569.

Shewhart, W. A. (1939). *Statistical method from the viewpoint of quality control.* The Graduate School, Department of Agriculture.

REFERENCES

Skillicorn, N. (2016, April 15). What is Innovation? 15 innovation experts give us their definition. Posted to the Internet. https://www.ideatovalue.com/inno/nickskillicorn/2016/03/innovation-15-experts

Skinner, B. F. (1953). *Science and human behavior.* Macmillan.

Smith, B. C. (2015). *How does learning agile business leadership differ? Exploring a revised model of the construct of learning agility in relation to executive performance.* [Unpublished doctoral dissertation]. Columbia University.

Smither, J. W., London, M., Flautt R., Vargas, Y., & Kucine, I. (2003). Can working with an executive coach improve multisource feedback ratings over time? A quasi-experimental field study. *Personnel Psychology, 56,* 23–44.

Spreitzer, G. M., McCall, M. W., & Mahoney, J. D. (1997). Early identification of international executive potential. *Journal of Applied Psychology, 82*(1), 6.

Stajkovic, A., & Luthans, F. (1997). A meta-analysis of the effects of organizational behavior modification on task performance, 1975-1995. *Academy of Management Journal, 40,* 1122–1149.

Thorndike, E. L. (1898). Animal Intelligence and experimental study of the association processes in animals. *Psychological Monograph, 8.*

Thorndike, E. L. (1908). The effect of practice in the case of a purely intellectual function. *American Journal of Psychology, 19,* 374–384.

Urick, T. (2017). *Insights.* Penguin Random House.

Vandewalle, D., & Cummings, L. L. (1997). A test of the influence of goal orientation on the feedback-seeking process. *Journal of Applied Psychology, 82,* 390–400.

Wiium, N., Aarø, L. E., & Hetland, J. (2009). Psychological reactance and adolescents' attitudes toward tobacco-control measures. *Journal of Applied Social Psychology, 39*(7), 1718–1738.

Yerkes, R. M., & Dodson, J. D. (1908). The relation of strength of stimulus to rapidity of habit formation. *Journal of Comparative Neurology and Psychology, 18*(5), 459–482.

ABOUT THE AUTHORS

DAVID F. HOFF

David F. Hoff is Chief Operating Officer and Executive Vice President of Leadership Development at EASI Consult, a position he has held since 2003. David leads organization transformation projects utilizing assessment and development expertise. David spent 17 years at Anheuser-Busch Companies, Inc. as Director of International Human Resources, Director of Human Resource Development and Selection, Manager of Management Development and Training and Organization Development Consultant. He's held corporate positions such as Vice President of Human Resources for Dimension Data, Inc. and Managing Director of International Human Resources for Proxicom, Inc. In addition to a deep background in management and organization development, David has 10 years of international experience in Asia, Latin America and Europe. David has over 25 years of experience in the identification and application of competencies, starting in the late 70s working with David McClelland at McBer and Company. He did his graduate work at Teachers College, Columbia University earning an M.A. and M.Ed. He lives in Wilmington, N.C. with his wife Susan.

W. WARNER BURKE

W. Warner Burke is the Emeritus Professor of Psychology and Education at Teachers College, Columbia University where he has been since 1979. Dr. Burke has authored or edited 20 books and written over 150 articles and book chapters. He has served as Editor of Organizational Dynamics, Academy of Management Executive, and the Journal of Applied Behavioral Science. He is a Fellow of the Academy of Management, Association of Psychological Science, the Society of Industrial and Organizational Psychology, and a Diplomate in industrial and organizational psychology, American Board of Professional Psychology. He has received several lifetime achievement awards, NASA's Public Service Medal, and The Outstanding Civilian Service Award from the Department of the Army.

INDEX

A

ability
  baseline, or starting point, 34, 83, 91, 96–97, 107, 137, 155
  defined, 88
  in *Feedback Seeking,* 146
  in *Flexibility,* 76, 81
  in *Information Gathering,* 143
  in *Performance Risk Taking,* 110
  in *Reflecting,* 158
  in *Speed,* 88, 93–94
accuracy, in *Speed,* 94, 97
acting, considering options before, 79–81
actions or events, considering reasons for and consequences of, 160–161
active listening, 150
actual (raw) scores, 6, 27
aggregated scores, 17–19
  highest and lowest scores, 17–18
  unrecognized strengths and blind spots, 18–19
agile learner, 52, 68–69, 71
agility, defined, 88
Agreeableness, 166
Amazon Mechanical Turk (MTurk), 57

ambiguity, tolerance for, 57, 59, 61, 62, 63, 67, 68
ambiguous tasks, engaging in, 114, 116, 118
analytic strategy, 60–63
approaches, trying different, 104–106
Argyris, Chris, 48, 50, 51–52
Arneson, Steve, 143, 155
assessment taker
  coach to help review and understand Burke results, 25–31
  leadership development program to provide feedback to, 22
  unrecognized strengths and blind spots of, 18–19

B

Barba, Jorge, 77, 84
baseline, or starting point, 34, 83, 91, 96–97, 107, 137, 155
Baumgartner, Jeffrey, 77, 84
behavioral descriptions
  Collaborating, 132–138
  Experimenting, 102–107
  Feedback Seeking, 147–155
  Flexibility, 76–86

behavioral descriptions
(*Continued*)
Information Gathering,
140–144
Interpersonal Risk Taking,
121–127
Performance Risk Taking,
112–120
Reflecting, 158–163
Speed, 88–99
See also individual descriptors
behaviorism, 48, 49–50
Big 5 dimensions, 58, 166
biodata inventory, 63
blind spots, 18–19
Bootstrap Leadership
(Arneson), 143
brainstorming, 75, 79–80, 81
Burke Learning Agility
assessments
multi-rater versions (*see* Burke multi-rater versions)
self-reports (*see* Burke self-report assessments)
validating through directive and nondirective coaching, 25–31
Burke Learning Agility Inventory (LAI) Expanded Version
dimension and item report, 13–14
LAI Standard Version differentiated from, 11
See also Burke self-report assessments

Burke Learning Agility Inventory (LAI) Standard Version
dimension report, example of, 13
LAI Expanded Version differentiated from, 11, 13
See also Burke self-report assessments
Burke Learning Agility Survey (LAS) 180
aggregated scores in, 17–19
LAS 360 differentiated from, 11
summary by learning agility dimension, 16
summary by learning agility dimension and by item, 19–20
See also Burke multi-rater versions
Burke Learning Agility Survey (LAS) 360
aggregated scores in, 17–19
LAS 180 differentiated from, 11
summary by learning agility dimension, 16–17
summary by learning agility dimension and by item, 20–21
See also Burke multi-rater versions
Burke multi-rater versions, 9, 14–23, 26–31
aggregated scores in, 17–19
components of, 15
differences between, 11
dimension level scoring, 15
dimensions of, defined, 4, 10

INDEX

information obtained by, 27
item scores by dimension, 29–30
Likert scale used in, 11
multi-rater feedback, 70, 153
open-ended questions in,
 22–23
organization of, 26
overview of, 5–6, 9, 14
results, prediction of, 27, 28–29
results, process for understanding
 and reviewing, 30–31
scales used in, 27
self-report assessments
 differentiated from, 11, 23
self-report questions in, 11
summary by learning agility
 dimension, 16–17
summary by learning agility
 dimension and by item,
 19–21
summary comments
 regarding, 22
summary of, 15
See also Burke Learning Agility
 Survey (LAS) 180; Burke
 Learning Agility Survey (LAS)
 360
Burke self-report assessments, 9,
 13–14, 23
 baseline, or starting point,
  34, 83, 91, 96–97, 107,
  137, 155
 differences between, 11, 13
 dimensions of, defined, 4, 10

information obtained by, 27
item scores by dimension,
 29–30
Likert scale used in, 11
multi-rater versions
 differentiated from, 11
normed, 11, 27
organization of, 26
output of, 13
overview of, 5, 9
profile by dimension, 12–13
psychometric properties of,
 55–57
research leading to, 6
results, process for understanding
 and reviewing, 27–30
sample overall score, 12
scales used in, 27
validating results, 27–30
See also Burke Learning Agility
 Inventory (LAI), Expanded
 Version; Burke Learning
 Agility Inventory (LAI)
 Standard Version
Burke's research, 6
Burke Suite of Learning Agility
 products, 9–10. *See also*
 individual products

C

capability. *See* ability
challenging roles, taking on, 113,
 115–116, 117–118
clutching, 98–99

179

coaching/coach, 25–31
coalition building, 66, 67, 69
cognitive ability, 26, 88, 91, 167
cognitive rigidity, 57, 59, 61, 62, 63
Collaborating, 130–138
   behavioral descriptions of (*see Collaborating* descriptors)
   defined, 4, 10
   Experimenting and, 104, 106, 107
   Flexibility and, 132, 134, 135
   importance of, 131
   Information Gathering and, 141, 142
   Interpersonal Risk Taking and, 133, 134, 135, 137
   in life example, 36–37, 40, 41
   networking in, 130, 131, 132
   overview of, 130–131
   in profile by dimension, 12
   Reflection and, 162
   scoring on, 15
   Speed and, 91, 94, 95–96
   stage 2 descriptive statistics and correlations, 62
Collaborating descriptors, 132–138
   asks stakeholders for their point of view, 137–138
   collaborates with other parts of the organization, 136–137
   leverages skills, knowledge, and talents of others, 132–133
   overview of, 132
   works with colleagues from different backgrounds, 134–136
colleagues from different backgrounds, working with, 134–136
communication, 66, 116, 130
composure, 66
computer-aided design (CAD), 39
Conscientiousness, 166
context
   in DeRue's model, 3–4, 75
   in *Flexibility*, 75
   importance of, 3–4
convergent validity, 58–59, 61, 62
courage, 66, 69, 128, 151, 155
criterion-related validity, 63–67
   measures of learning agility, 63–64
   performance, 65
   results and discussion, 65–67
   sample and procedure, 63
Cronbach's alpha, 55
Croson, Rick, 34–43. *See also* life example of learning agility
culture, organization's, 75
customer, in innovation, 77–78

D

data
   collecting, to increase knowledge and inform next steps, 143–144

defined, 143
performance, in criterion-related validity, 65
da Vinci, Leonardo, 68
defensive reactions, 48
Deming, William Edwards, 158
Deming cycle of continuous process improvement, 158, 159
DeRue, D. S., 3–5, 52, 55, 73, 75
DeRue's model of learning agility
  antecedents in, 4
  context in, 3–4, 75
  Speed and *Flexibility* in, 4–5, 52, 74
descriptors. *See* behavioral descriptions
dimensions
  codes for, in life example of learning agility, 42–43
  Collaborating, 130–138
  defined, 4, 10
  Experimenting, 102–107
  Feedback Seeking, 146–156
  Flexibility, 74–86
  Information Gathering, 140–144
  Interpersonal Risk Taking, 120–128
  item scores by, 29–30
  level scoring, in multi-rater versions, 15
  Performance Risk Taking, 110–120
  profile by, 12–13
  Reflecting, 158–163
  Speed, 88–99
  summary by item, in multi-rater versions, 19–21
  summary of, in multi-rater versions, 16–17
  See also individual dimensions
discriminant validity, 57, 59–63
disorganized task force example, 124–126
Dodson, John Dillingham, 98
double-loop learning, 48, 50–52

E

E.A.S.I-Consult, 6, 9, 25, 131
effective, reflecting on how to be more, 160
ego resilience, 57, 58, 61, 62, 63
errors
  in *Experimenting*, 106–107
  in *Speed*, 90
Eurich, Tasha, 151, 153, 155
events, evaluating, 162–163
execution capability, 66
Experimenting, 102–107
  behavioral descriptions of (*see Experimenting* descriptors)
  Collaborating and, 104, 106, 107
  defined, 4, 10
  feedback in, 103, 105–106
  Feedback Seeking and, 106, 107
  final thoughts on, 107
  Flexibility in, 103–104, 159
  and *Information Gathering*, 144

Experimenting (Conitnued)
   in life example, 36, 37–38, 39, 40
   Performance Risk Taking compared to, 102, 107
   Reflecting and, 107
   scoring on, 15
   Speed and, 91
   stage 2 descriptive statistics and correlations, 62
Experimenting descriptors, 102–107
   evaluates new ways of solving problems, 102–103
   experiments with unproven ideas, 103–104
   learns by trial and error, 106–107
   tries different approaches, 104–106
external locus of control, 56–57, 63, 166

F

feedback
   coach for providing, 25–26, 29
   in *Experimenting*, 103, 105–106
   in *Flexibility*, 82, 85
   importance of, for learning agility, 47, 49, 50, 56, 63, 68, 70, 71, 85
   to improve interactions, 150–151
   in *Interpersonal Risk Taking*, 122
   leadership development program for providing, 22
   on performance, asking peers for, 154–155
   in *Reflecting*, 160, 161
   seeking from others, 147–151
   for skill and motivation, 5, 26, 89
   in *Speed*, 89, 95–96, 97
   understanding, 149–151
   See also Feedback Seeking
Feedback Seeking, 146–156
   defined, 4, 10, 147
   Experimenting and, 106, 107
   final thoughts on, 155–156
   Information Gathering and, 141
   in LAS 180 report, 19–20
   in LAS 360 report, 20–21
   from others, 147–151
   overview of, 146
   in profile by dimension, 12
   scoring on, 15
   self-awareness in, 148
   Speed and, 91, 94
   stage 2 descriptive statistics and correlations, 62
   ways of demonstrating, 147
Feedback Seeking descriptors, 147–155
   asks others how to improve performance, 154–155
   asks peers for feedback on performance, 154–155
   discussing advancement with your supervisor, 151–154
   seeking feedback from others, 147–151

Flexibility, 74–86
  behavioral descriptions of (*see Flexibility* descriptors)
  Burke's definition of, 74–75
  Collaborating and, 132, 134, 135
  context in, 75
  defined, 4, 10
  in DeRue's model of learning agility, 4–5, 52, 74
  Experimenting and, 103–104, 159
  feedback in, 82, 85
  final thoughts on, 86
  idea generation in, 75
  importance of, in learning agility, 4–5, 88–89
  Interpersonal Risk Taking and, 127, 128
  in LAI Expanded Version, 13–14
  in LAS 180 report, 16, 19
  in LAS 360 report, 17
  in life example, 35, 36, 37, 38, 39, 40, 41
  openness to new ideas, 74–76
  paradigm shift in, 92
  Performance Risk Taking and, 119, 120
  Reflecting and, 159
  Speed and, 92, 97
  in Spider Diagram from Burke Report, 15
  stage 2 descriptive statistics and correlations, 62

Flexibility descriptors, 76–86
  articulates competing ideas/perspectives, 85–86
  considers options before acting, 79–81
  finds common themes, 83–85
  overview of, 76
  paradigm shift in, 92
  proposes innovative solutions, 77–79
  switches among different tasks/jobs, 82–83
force, promoting and restraining, 80–81
Force Field Analysis, 80, 81

G
Gallwey, Tim, 97
global mindset, 66
Grant, Adam, 135–136

H
habit, 89, 91, 94, 95, 97, 98
help, asking others for, 123, 125

I
ideas
  challenges others,' even when they are shared by many, 124, 126
  evaluation of, 80
  experiments with unproven, 103–104
ideas/concepts, in *Speed*, 95–96

ideas/perspectives, in *Flexibility*
  articulating competing, 85–86
  generation of, 75
independent variable, 105
inductive reasoning, 79
information
  reading journals, books, etc. to stay informed, 142–143
  on topics related to field, 140–141
Information Gathering, 140–144
  behavioral descriptions of (*see Information Gathering* descriptors)
  Collaborating and, 141, 142
  defined, 4, 10
  Experimenting and, 144
  Feedback Seeking and, 141
  final thoughts on, 144
  Interpersonal Risk Taking and, 141
  in life example, 35, 36–37, 38, 40, 41
  methods of, 27
  overview of, 140
  scoring on, 15
  Speed and, 91, 94, 95
  stage 2 descriptive statistics and correlations, 62
Information Gathering descriptors, 140–144
  collects data to increase knowledge and inform next steps, 143–144
  overview of, 140
  reads journals, books, etc. to stay informed, 142–143
  seeks new information on topics related to their field, 140–141
  updates knowledge through training and education, 141–142
Inner Game of Tennis, The (Gallwey), 97
innovation, 66, 77–79
  definitions of, 77, 84
  paradigm shift in, 92
  scales to quantify innovativeness, 78–79
  themes in, 77–78
Insight (Eurich), 151
inspirational leadership, 65, 66, 67, 69
integrity and trust, 66
intellectual capacity, 66, 67
international assignment example, 115–117
Interpersonal Risk Taking, 120–128
  behavioral descriptions of (*see Interpersonal Risk Taking* descriptors)
  Collaborating and, 133, 134, 135, 137
  defined, 4, 10, 110
  feedback in, 122
  final thoughts on, 128
  Flexibility and, 127, 128

Information Gathering and, 141
in life example, 35, 36, 37, 40
overview of, 120–121
in profile by dimension, 12
Reflecting and, 127, 161, 162
scoring on, 15
self-awareness in, 120, 128
Speed and, 91, 94, 96, 127
stage 2 descriptive statistics and correlations, 62
Interpersonal Risk Taking
descriptors, 121–127
asks others for help, 123, 125
brings up tough issues with others, 123, 125
challenges others' ideas even when they are shared by many, 124, 126
discusses mistakes with others, 124, 126
in disorganized task force example, 124–126
overview of, 121–123
in senior management conference example, 123–124
issues, bringing up with others, 123, 125
items
of *Flexibility,* 76–86
generation and reduction, 54–55
reliability, 55
report of, 13–14
scores by dimension, 29–30
summary by, 19–21

J
judgment, 63, 66, 67, 69, 75

K
Kadushin, Charles, 130
Kahneman, Daniel, 88–91, 93, 97, 99
knowledge
collecting data to increase, 143–144
knowledge-in-action, 52
leveraging, 132–133
Speed and, 93–94, 96–97
updating through training and education, 141–142
knowledge, skills, and abilities (KSAs), 93–94

L
laboratory method, 48–49
LAI Expanded Version. *See* Burke Learning Agility Inventory (LAI), Expanded Version
LAI Standard Version. *See* Burke Learning Agility Inventory (LAI) Standard Version
LAS 180. *See* Burke Learning Agility Survey (LAS) 180
LAS 360. *See* Burke Learning Agility Survey (LAS) 360
leader development, 23, 46–47, 63
leader selection and development, 46–48

Leadership Excellence Framework (LEF), 65
learning ability, distinguished from learning agility, 4
learning agility
   Burke assessments on, 5–6
   Burke's research on, 6
   defined, 26
   DeRue's model of, 3–5, 52, 74, 75
   dimensions of, defined, 4, 10
   effect of "context" or environment on, 26
   leadership competencies and, 66
   learning ability distinguished from, 4
   life example of, 34–43
   overview of, 6–7
   skill and motivation in, 5, 26
   theory and research on, 45–71
Learning Agility: The Key to Leader Potential (Hoff and Burke), 1, 3, 5–7, 165
learning goal orientation, 56, 57, 58, 61, 62, 63, 67
Lewin, Kurt, 48, 80
life example of learning agility, 34–43
   building the perfect boat, 38–39
   building the perfect lure, 36–38
   codes for dimensions in, 42–43
   Collaborating and, 36–37, 40, 41
   continuing to learn and grow, 40–41
   Experimenting and, 36, 37–38, 39, 40
   Flexibility and, 35, 36, 37, 38, 39, 40, 41
   Information Gathering and, 35, 36–37, 38, 40, 41
   Interpersonal Risk Taking and, 35, 36, 37, 40
   opportunistically responding to new market demands, 39–40
   overview of, 34–36
   Performance Risk Taking and, 34–35, 39–40, 41
   Reflecting and, 36, 37, 39, 40, 41
   Speed and, 35, 39–40, 41
Likert scale, 11, 53, 58, 59, 60
locus of control, 59–63, 67
   chance, 59, 61, 62
   external, 56–57, 63, 166
   powerful others, 59, 61, 62

M

Management Development Panel, 82
McFarthing, Kevin, 77, 84
means, 54, 55
measures of learning agility, 58–60
   behaviorism, 49–50
   convergent validity, 58–59, 61, 62
   criterion-related validity, 63–64
   developing, 48–52
   discriminant validity, 59–60, 61–63

double-loop learning and Reflection, 50–52
meaning of, 68–69
T-Group theory, 48–49
motivation, 5, 26
multitasking, 82, 86

N

networking
  in *Collaborating,* 130, 131, 132
  in *Information Gathering,* 141
neuroticism, 166
new tasks/projects, getting up to speed on, 93–95
normative (norm) group, 11
normed Burke self-report assessments, 11, 27

O

observation, information obtained by, 27
Occupational Personality Questionnaire (OPQ-32), 63
openness to experience, 55, 57, 58, 61, 62, 63, 166
Openness to New Experiences, Hogan's, 166
operant behavior, 49–50
Oreg's Resistance to Change scale, 59
organization
  collaborating with, 136–137
  culture of, 75

other rater score, 11, 15, 16–18, 20, 27, 29, 30–31
outliers, 91

P

paradigm shift, 92–93
performance
  asking peers for feedback on, 154–155
  data, in criterion-related validity, 65
  pressure and, relationship between, 98
performance rating, 63, 64, 65
performance risk framework, 113–115
Performance Risk Taking, 110–120
  behavioral descriptions of (*see Performance Risk Taking* descriptors)
  defined, 4, 10, 110
  Experimenting compared to, 102, 107
  final thoughts on, 119–120
  Flexibility and, 119, 120
  international assignment example, 115–117
  level of risk and, 110–111, 115
  in life example, 34–35, 39–40, 41
  overall, 113, 114, 117
  performance risk framework, 113–115
  in profile by dimension, 12

Performance Risk Taking
(*Continued*)
   reducing assignment's challenges, 117–119
   Reflecting and, 119, 120
   scoring on, 15
   Speed and, 94, 96, 118–119, 120
   stage 2 descriptive statistics and correlations, 62
   time and resources in, 111–112
Performance Risk Taking descriptors, 112–120
   embraces work that is risky, 114, 116, 118
   engages in ambiguous tasks, 114, 116, 118
   in international assignment example, 115–117
   overview of, 112–113
   in performance risk framework, 113–115
   in reducing the assignment's challenges, 117–119
   takes on challenging roles, 113, 115–116, 117–118
   volunteers for projects that involve the possibility of failure, 114, 116–117, 118–119
Plan, Do, Plan, Do, Plan, Do, 158
Plan, Do, Study, and Act, 158, 159
Potential Leader Development Center (PLDC), 63, 64, 65
pressure and performance, relationship between, 98
problems
   evaluating new ways of solving, 102–103
   unexpected, reacting well to, 98–99
profile by dimension, 12–13
projects involving possible failure, volunteering for, 114, 116–117, 118–119
Project Talent, 130
psychometric properties of LAI, 55–57

Q
qualifiers, 29
questions
   open-ended, 22
   self-report, 11

R
ratings, performance, 64
Raven's Progressive Matrices, 63
raw (actual) scores, 6, 27
reactance, 57, 60, 61, 62, 63
Reflecting, 158–163
   behavioral descriptions of (*see Reflecting* descriptors)
   Collaborating and, 162
   defined, 4, 10
   Experimenting and, 107
   feedback in, 160, 161
   Feedback Seeking and, 160, 161

final thoughts on, 163
Flexibility and, 159
Interpersonal Risk Taking and, 127, 162
in life example, 36, 37, 39, 40, 41
Performance Risk Taking and, 119, 120
scoring on, 15
self-awareness in, 160–161
Speed and, 91, 94–95, 97
stage 2 descriptive statistics and correlations, 62
Reflecting descriptors, 158–163
considers reasons for and consequences of actions or events, 160–161
evaluates events with others to understand what happened, 162–163
overview of, 158
reflects on how to be more effective, 160
reflects on work processes and projects, 159
reflection, double-loop learning and, 50–52
reflection-in-action, 51–52
reflective practice, 51–52
reliability, 54, 55
research, Burke's, 6
resistance to change, 59, 62
resources, in *Performance Risk Taking*, 111–112
results, prediction of, 27, 28–29

risk
concept of, 110
level of, 110–111, 115
quantifying, 122–123
at work, embracing, 114, 116, 118
See also Interpersonal Risk Taking; Performance Risk Taking
risk aversion, 57, 60, 61, 62, 63

S

scales, to quantify innovativeness, 78–79
Schön, Donald, 48, 50, 51–52
scores
aggregated, 17–19
distribution of, across all participants, 23
highest and lowest, 17–18
item, by dimension, 29–30
other rater, 11, 15, 16–18, 20, 27, 29, 30–31
overall, 12
PLDC, 63, 64, 65
raw (actual), 6, 27
self-rated, 15, 18, 19, 29, 30, 146
unrecognized strengths and blind spots, 18–19
self, in *Speed,* experiencing and remembering, 91
self-affirmation, 151

self-awareness, 23, 46
  in *Feedback Seeking*, 148
  in *Interpersonal Risk Taking*, 120, 128
  in *Reflecting*, 160–161
  in T-group theory, 48, 49
self-efficacy, 58, 62
self-rated score, 15, 18, 19, 29, 30, 146
self-report
  information obtained by, 27
  questions, 11
senior management conference example, 123–124
sensitivity training, 48–49
70-20-10 rule of leader development, 47
single-loop learning, 48, 50–51
situational judgment test, 63
Skillicorn, Nick, 77, 84
skills, 5, 26
  in *Collaborating*, leveraging, 132–133
  in *Speed*, 89–90, 93–94, 96–97
Skinner, B. F., 48, 49, 50
solutions
  developing, in *Speed*, 91–93
  proposing innovative, in *Flexibility*, 77–79
Spearman correlation, 64, 65
Speed, 88–99
  abilities in, 93–94
  accuracy in, 94, 97

behavioral descriptions of (*see Speed* descriptors)
cognitive ability and, 88, 91
Collaborating and, 91, 94, 95–96
defined, 4, 10, 99
in DeRue's model of learning agility, 4–5, 52, 74
errors and, 90
Experimenting and, 91
feedback in, 89, 95–96, 97
Feedback Seeking and, 91, 94
final thoughts on, 99
Flexibility and, 92, 97
habit and, 89, 91, 94, 95, 97, 98
importance of, in learning agility, 4–5, 88–89
Information Gathering and, 91, 94, 95
Interpersonal Risk Taking and, 91, 94, 96, 127
Kahneman's ideas on, 88–91, 93, 97, 99
knowledge in, 93–94, 96–97
in LAS 180 report, 16, 19
in LAS 360 report, 17
in life example, 35, 39–40, 41
other dimensions in, 94–95
paradigm shift in, 92–93
Performance Risk Taking and, 94, 118–119, 120
Reflecting and, 91, 94–95, 97
self in, experiencing and remembering, 91
skill in, 89–90, 93–94, 96–97

in Spider Diagram from Burke Report, 15
stage 2 descriptive statistics and correlations, 62
Speed descriptors, 88–99
  acquires new skills and knowledge rapidly, 96–97
  gets up to speed on new tasks/projects, 93–95
  overview of, 88–91
  quickly develops solutions, 91–93
  reacts well to unexpected problems, 98–99
  readily grasps new ideas/concepts, 95–96
Spider Diagram from Burke Report, 15
stakeholders, asking for their point of view, 137–138
stamina, 66
standard deviations, 54, 55
strategic agility, 66, 67, 69
strengths, unrecognized, 18–19
System 1, Kahneman's, 89–91, 94, 95, 97, 99
System 2, Kahneman's, 89–90, 97, 99

T

talent management, 65, 66, 67, 69, 105
talents in *Collaborating*, leveraging, 132–133
tasks/jobs, switching among different, 82–83
themes in *Flexibility,* finding common, 83–85, 103, 119, 127, 159
theory and research on learning agility, 45–71
  analytic strategy, 60–63
  behaviorism, 49–50
  convergent validity, 58–59, 61, 62
  criterion-related validity, 63–67
  discriminant validity, 59–63
  double-loop learning and reflection, 50–52
  general discussion, 67–69
  implications, 70–71
  introduction, 45
  item generation and reduction, 54–55
  leader selection and development, 46–48
  limitations, 70
  main conceptual categories for, 52–53
  measures of learning agility, 48–52, 58–60, 63–64
  performance data, 65
  performance ratings and, 64
  psychometric properties of LAI, 55–57
  reliability, 55
  results and discussion, 65–67
  sample and procedure, 57, 63
  T-Group theory, 48–49

Think Again: The Power of Knowing What You Don't Know (Grant), 135–136
Thinking, Fast and Slow (Kahneman), 88–89
Thorndike, Edward Lee, 48, 106
time, in *Performance Risk Taking*, 111–112
tolerance for ambiguity, 57, 59, 61, 62, 63, 67, 68
Training-Group (T-Group) theory, 48–49
trial and error, learning by, 106–107

U

unchartered waters, 34
understanding feedback, 149–151
unrecognized strengths, 18–19

V

validity
  of Burke assessment, 25–31
  convergent, 58–59, 61, 62
  criterion-related, 63–64
  discriminant, 59–63
value, in innovation, 77–78
van Wulfen, Gijs, 77, 84
volunteering for projects involving possible failure, 114, 116–117, 118–119

W

work processes and projects, reflecting on, 159

Y

Yerkes, Robert, 98
Yerkes-Dodson law, 98